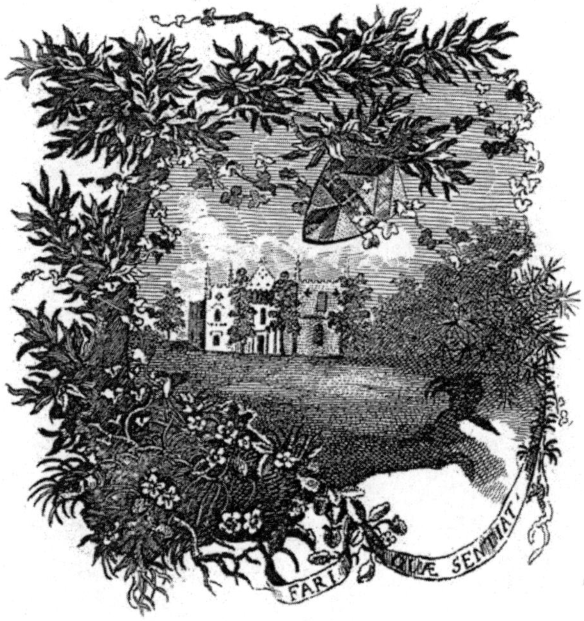
FARI QUÆ SENTIAT

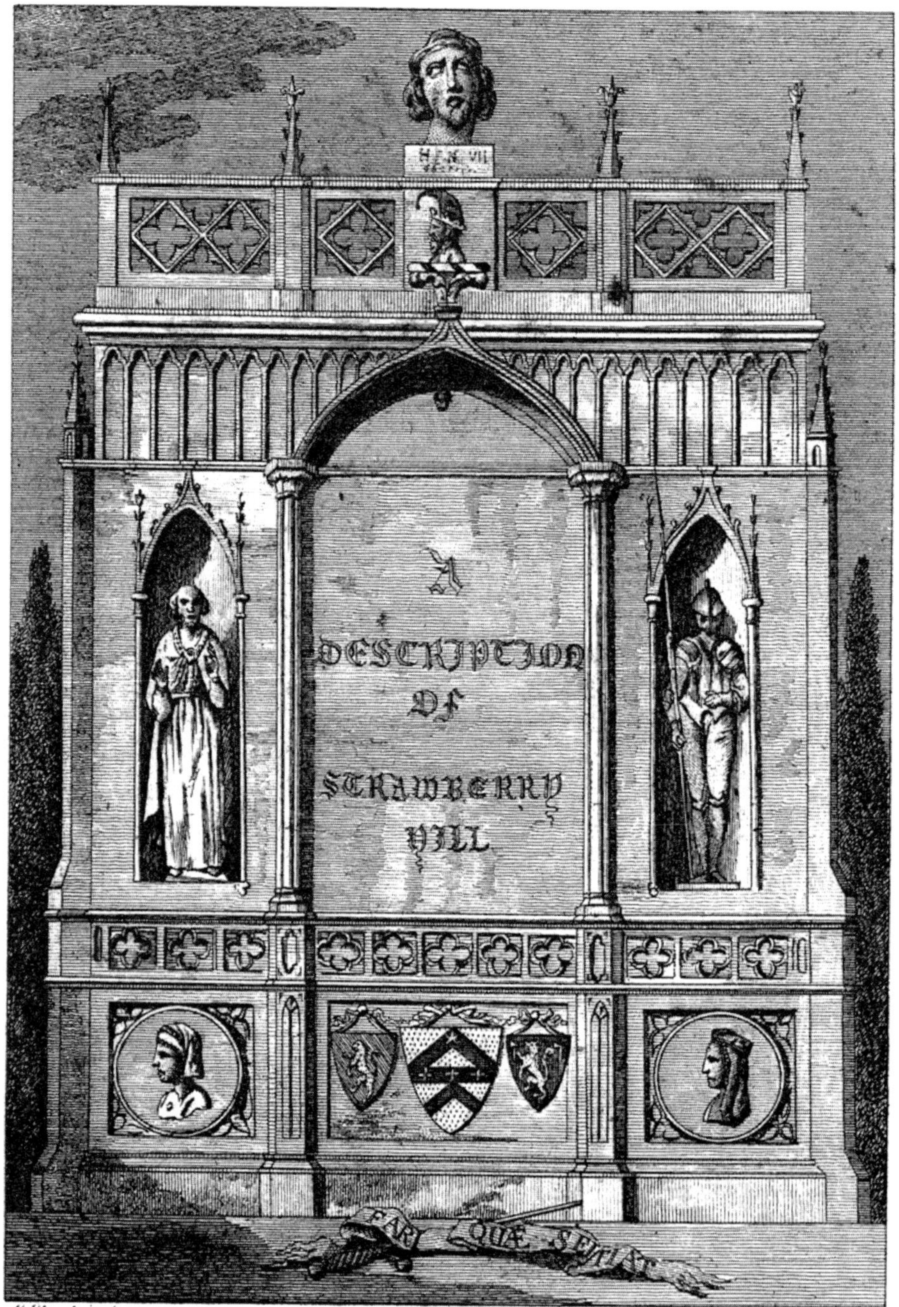

E. Edwards inv. Morris fc.

FRONTISPIECE.

A

DESCRIPTION

OF THE

VILLA

OF

Mr. HORACE WALPOLE,

AT

Strawberry-Hill near Twickenham, Middlefex.

WITH AN INVENTORY OF THE

FURNITURE, PICTURES, CURIOSITIES, &c.

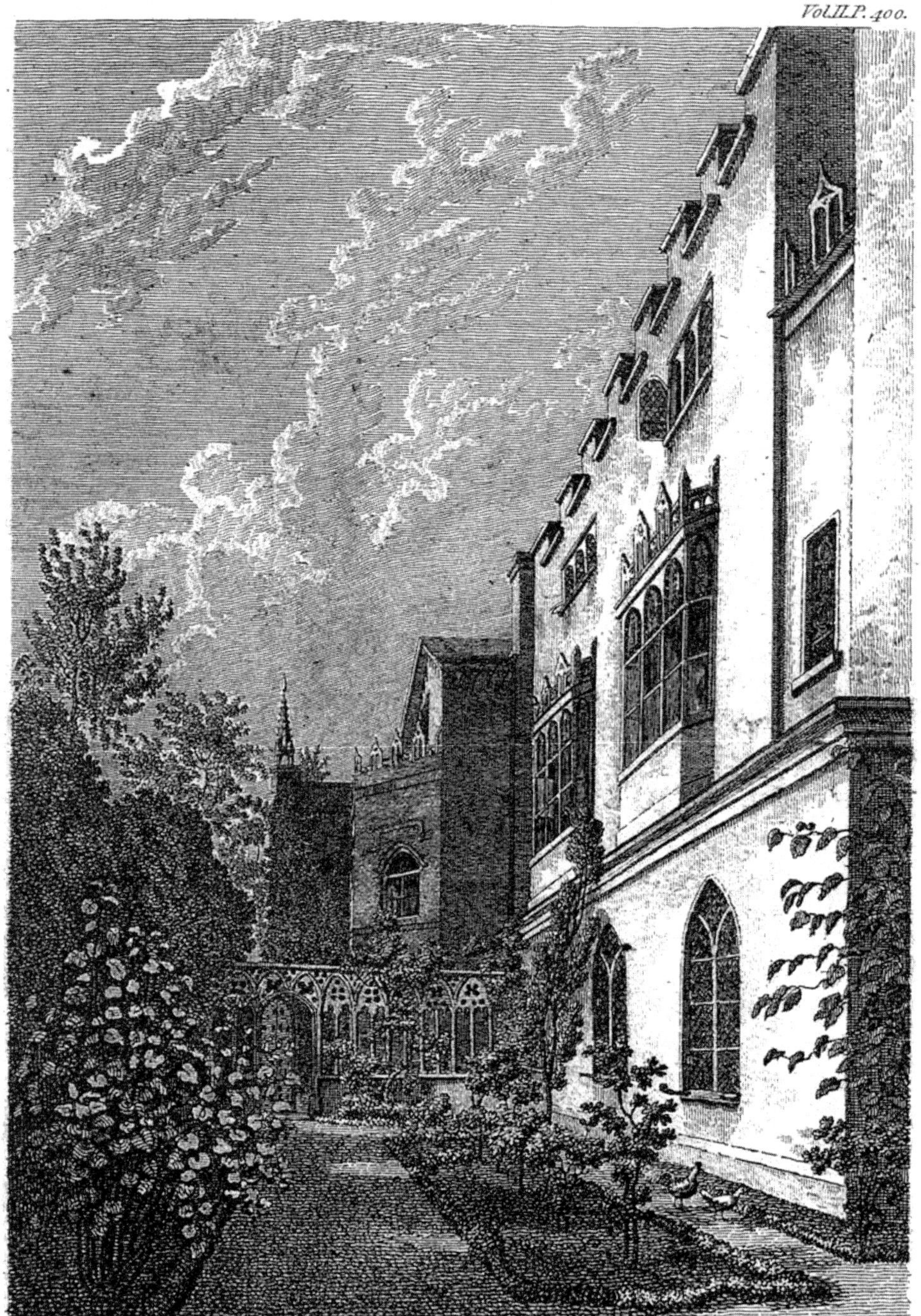

Parry del. Jeffrey Sc.

View of the Prior's Garden
AT STRAWBERRYHILL.

P R E F A C E.

IT will look, I fear, a little like arrogance in a private man to give a printed deſcription of his villa and collection, in which almoſt every thing is diminutive. It is not, however, intended for public ſale, and originally was meant only to aſſiſt thoſe who ſhould viſit the place. A farther view ſucceeded; that of exhibiting ſpecimens of Gothic architecture, as collected from ſtandards in cathedrals and chapel-tombs, and ſhowing how they may be applied to chimney-pieces, ceilings, windows, baluſtrades, loggias, &c. The general diſuſe of Gothic architecture, and the decay and alterations ſo frequently made in churches, give prints a chance of being the ſole preſervatives of that ſtyle.

Catalogues raiſonnés of collections are very frequent in France and Holland; and it is no high degree of vanity to aſſume for an exiſting collection an illuſtration that is allowed to many a temporary auction—an exiſting collection—even that phraſe is void of vanity. Having lived, unhappily, to ſee the nobleſt ſchool of painting that this kingdom beheld, tranſported almoſt out of the ſight of Europe, it would be ſtrange faſcination, nay, a total inſenſibility to the pride of family, and to the moral reflections that wounded pride commonly feels, to expect that a paper fabric and an aſſemblage of curious trifles, made by an inſignificant man, ſhould laſt or be treated with more veneration and reſpect than the trophies of a palace depoſited in it by one of the beſt and wiſeſt miniſters that this country has enjoyed.

Far from ſuch viſions of ſelf-love, the following account of pictures and rarities is given with a view to their future diſperſion. The ſeveral purchaſers will find a hiſtory of their purchaſes; nor do virtuoſos diſlike to refer to ſuch a catalogue for an authentic certificate of their curioſities. The following collection was made out of the ſpoils of many renowned cabinets; as Dr. Meade's, lady Elizabeth Germaine's, lord Oxford's, the ducheſs of Portland's, and of about forty more of celebrity. Such well-atteſted deſcent is the genealogy of the objects of virtù—not ſo noble as thoſe of the peerage, but on a par with thoſe of race-horſes. In all three, eſpecially the pedigrees of peers and rarities, the line is often continued by many inſignificant names.

The moſt conſiderable part of the following catalogue conſiſts of miniatures, enamels, and portraits of remarkable perſons. The collection of miniatures and enamels is, I believe, the largeſt and fineſt in any country. His Majeſty has ſome very fine, the duke of Portland more; in no other is to be ſeen, in any good preſervation, any number of the works of Iſaac and Peter Oliver. The large pieces by the latter, in the royal collection, faded long ago by being expoſed to the ſun and air. Monſ. Henery at Paris, and others, have many fine pieces of Petitot. In the following liſt are ſome moſt capital works of that maſter, and of his only rival Zincke. Raphael's miſſal is an unique work in miniature of that monarch of painting; and the book of pſalms by Julio Clovio the fineſt ſpecimen extant of illumination. The drawings and bas-reliefs in wax, by lady Diana Beauclerc, are as invaluable as rare.

To an Engliſh antiquary muſt be dear ſo many hiſtoric pictures of our ancient monarchs and royal family; no fewer than four family-pieces of Henry V, VI, VII, and VIII. of queen Mary Tudor and Charles Brandon; of the ducheſs of Suffolk and her ſecond huſband; and that curious and well-painted picture of Charles II. and his gardener. Nor will ſo many

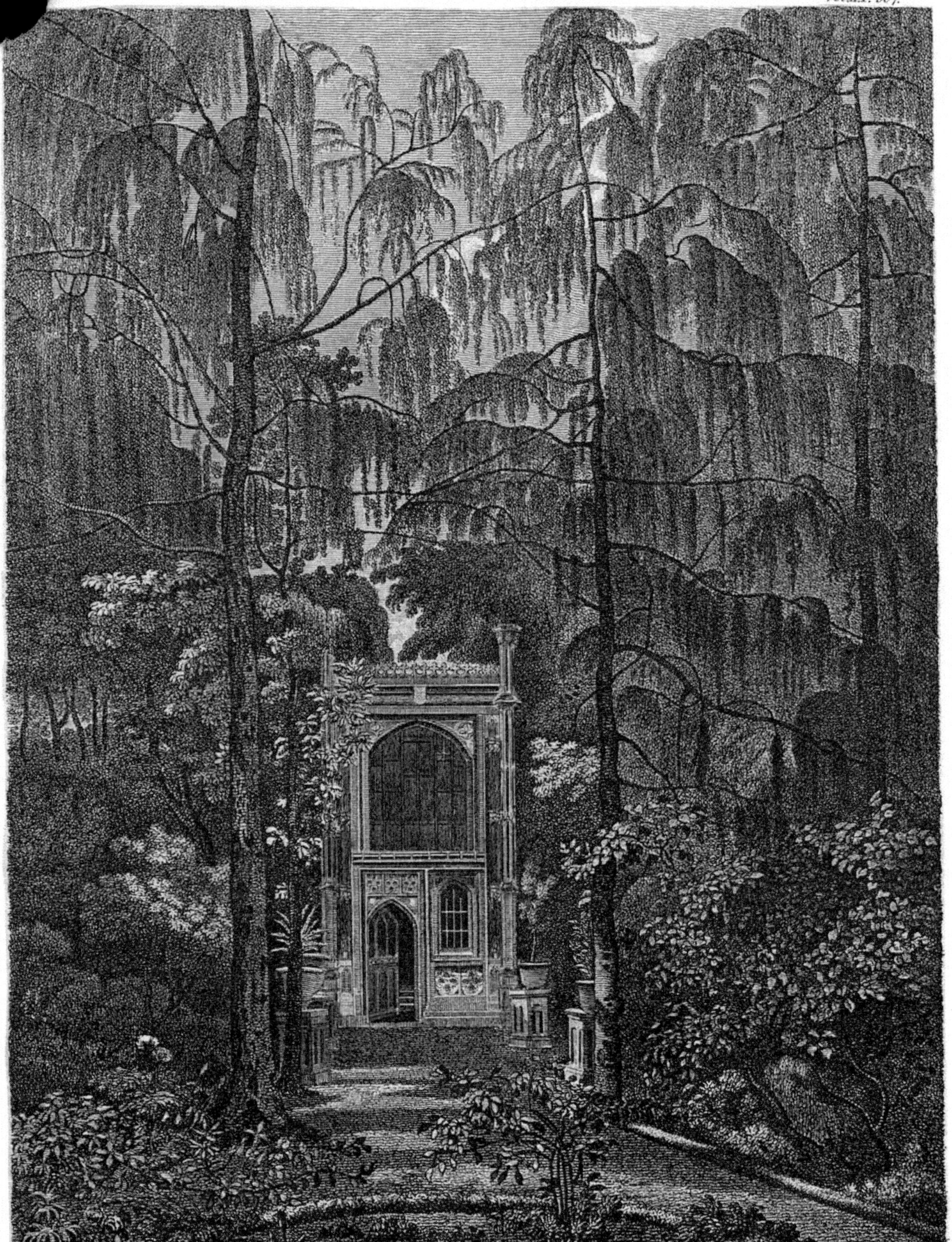

Pars delin. Godfrey Sc.

View of the Chapel in the Garden
at Strawberry hill.

works of Holbein be lefs precious to him, efpecially Zucchero's drawings from his Triumphs of Riches and Poverty.

To virtuofos of more claffic tafte, the fmall bufts of Jupiter Serapis in bafaltes, and of Caligula in bronze, and the filver bell of Benvenuto Cellini, will difplay the art of ancient and modern fculpture—how high it was carried by Greek ftatuaries, appears in the eagle.

To thofe who have ftill more tafte than confifts in mere fight, the catalogue itfelf will convey fatisfaction, by containing a copy of madame du Deffand's letter in the name of madame de Sevigné; not written in imitation of that model of letter-writers, but compofed of more delicacy of thought and more elegance of expreffion than perhaps madame de Sevigné herfelf could have attained. The two ladies ought not to be compared—one was all natural eafe and tendernefs—the other charms by the graces of the moft polifhed ftyle, which, however, are lefs beautiful than the graces of the wit they clothe.

Upon the whole, fome tranfient pleafure may even hereafter arife to the perufer of this catalogue. To others it may afford another kind of fatiffaction, that of criticifm. In a houfe affecting not only obfolete architecture, but pretending to an obfervance of the *coftume* even in the furniture, the mixture of modern portraits, and French porcelaine, and Greek and Roman fculpture, may feem heterogeneous. In truth, I did not mean to make my houfe fo Gothic as to exclude convenience, and modern refinements in luxury. The defigns of the infide and outfide are ftrictly ancient, but the decorations are modern*. Would our anceftors, before the reformation of architecture, not have depofited in their gloomy caftles antique ftatues

* And the mixture may be denominated, in fome words of Pope,

A Gothic Vatican of Greece and Rome.

and fine pictures, beautiful vases and ornamental china, if they had possessed them?—But I do not mean to defend by argument a small capricious house. It was built to please my own taste, and in some degree to realize my own visions. I have specified what it contains: could I describe the gay but tranquil scene where it stands, and add the beauty of the landscape to the romantic cast of the mansion, it would raise more pleasing sensations than a dry list of curiosities can excite: at least the prospect would recall the good humour of those who might be disposed to condemn the fantastic fabric, and to think it a very proper habitation of, as it was the scene that inspired, the author of the Castle of Otranto.

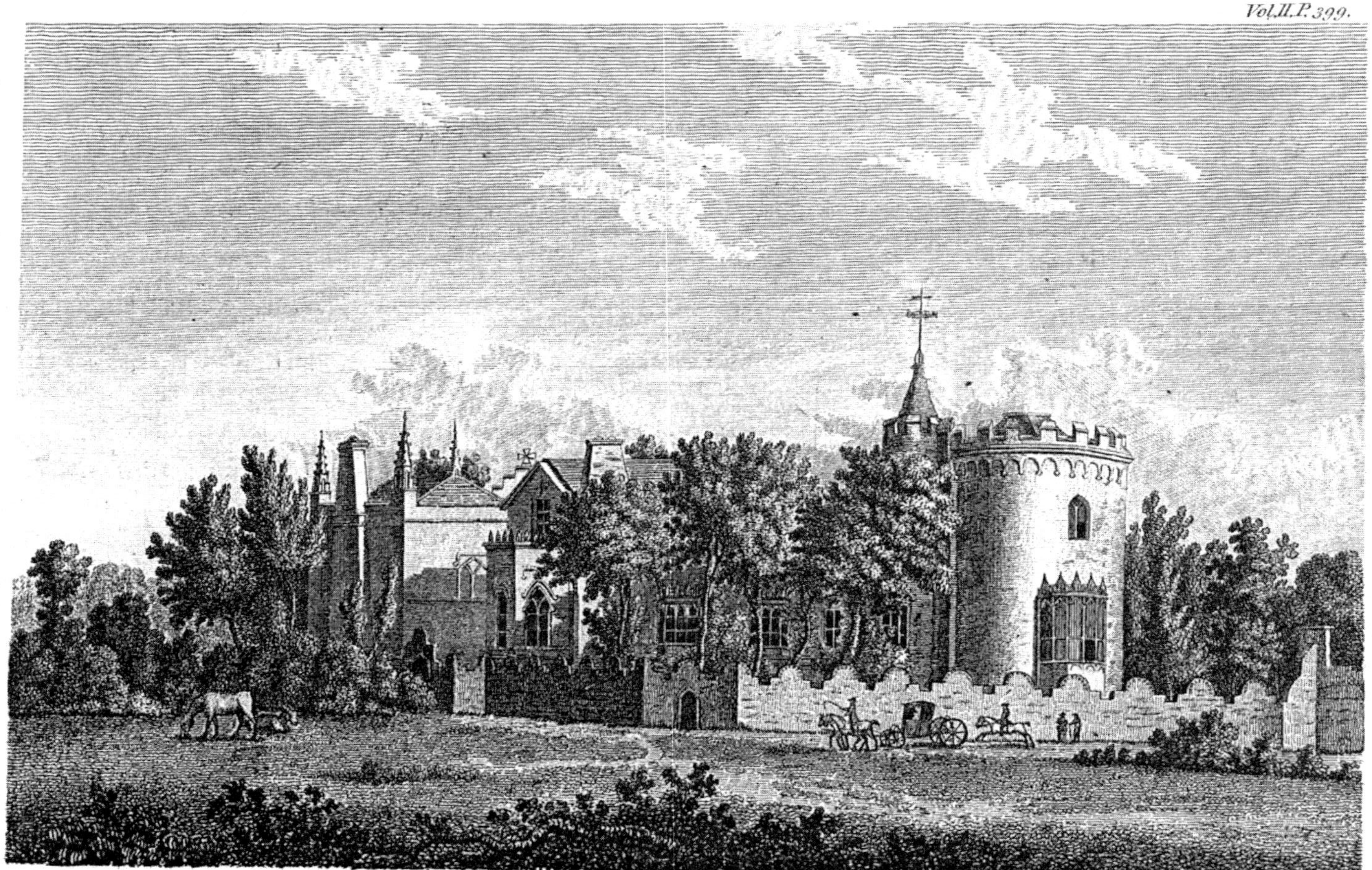

Marlow del. Godfrey Sc.

North Front of Strawberry hill.

A DESCRIPTION OF THE VILLA OF Mr. HORACE WALPOLE, AT STRAWBERRY-HILL NEAR TWICKENHAM.

WHERE the Gothic caſtle now ſtands, was originally a ſmall tenement *, built in 1698, and let as a lodging-houſe: Cibber once took it, and wrote one of his plays here, *The Refuſal, or the Lady's Philoſophy*. After him, Talbot biſhop of Durham had it for eight years †: then, Henry Bridges marquis of Carnarvon, ſon of James duke of Chandos, and ſince duke himſelf. It was next hired by Mrs. Chenevix ‡, the noted toy-woman, who, on the death of her huſband, let it to lord John Philip Sackville, ſecond ſon of Lionel duke of Dorſet: he kept it about two years, and then Mr. Walpole took the remainder of Mrs. Chenevix's leaſe in May 1747, and the next year bought it by act of parliament, it being the property of three minors of the name of Mortimer. Along with this houſe and ſome

* It was built by the earl of Bradford's coachman, and was called by the common people, *Chopp'd-Straw-Hall*, they ſuppoſing, that by feeding his lord's horſes with chopped ſtraw, he had ſaved money enough to build his houſe; but the piece of ground on which it ſtands is called in all the old leaſes, *Strawberry-Hill-Shot*, from whence it takes its name.

† The biſhop kept a large table here; which is ſcarce conceivable, as he had no kitchen but that little place which is now the china-room.

‡ Pere Courayer lodged here with her for ſome time.

other

other tenements was another ſmall one*, then occupied by Richard Francklin, printer of The Craftſman, who had been taken up for printing that paper during the adminiſtration of ſir Robert Walpole †. When Mr. Walpole bought Strawberry-hill, there were but five acres belonging to the houſe: the reſt have been purchaſed ſince. The caſtle now exiſting was not entirely built from the ground, but formed at different times, by alterations of and additions to the old ſmall houſe. The library, and refectory or great parlour, were entirely new built in 1753; the gallery, round tower, great cloiſter, and cabinet, in 1760 and 1761; the great north bed-chamber in 1770; and the Beauclerc tower with the hexagon cloſet in 1776.

The embattled wall to the road is taken from a print of Aſton-houſe in Warwickſhire, in Dugdale's hiſtory of that county.

Entering by the great north gate, the firſt object that preſents itſelf is a ſmall oratory encloſed with iron rails; in front, an altar, on which ſtands a ſaint in bronze; open niches, and ſtone baſons for holy water; deſigned by John Chute, eſq. of the Vine in Hampſhire. On the right hand is a ſmall garden called the abbot's garden, parted off by an open ſcreen, taken from the tomb of Roger Niger biſhop of London in old St. Paul's. Paſſing on the left, by a ſmall cloiſter‡, is the entrance to the houſe, the narrow front of which was deſigned by Richard Bentley, only ſon of Dr. Bentley, the learned maſter of Trinity-college, Cambridge. Over the door are three ſhields of Walpole, Shorter and Robſart.

* It has ſince been pulled down, and a cottage built on the ſame ſpot. The garden too has been newly laid out by Mr. Walpole ſince it came into his hands by Francklin's death.

† It is remarkable, that the printer of The Craftſman was Mr. Walpole's tenant; and that the writer of The Craftſman, W. Pulteney earl of Bath, wrote a ballad in praiſe of Strawberry-hill.

‡ In this cloiſter are two blue and white Delft flower-pots; and a bas-relief head in marble, inſcribed Dia Helianora: it is the portrait of the princeſs Eleanora d'Eſte, with whom Taſſo was in love, and who was the cauſe of his misfortunes: it was ſent to Mr. Walpole from Italy by ſir William Hamilton, miniſter at Naples. On a pedeſtal ſtands the large blue and white china tub in which Mr. Walpole's cat was drowned; on a label of the pedeſtal is written the firſt ſtanza of Mr. Gray's beautiful ode on that occaſion:

'Twas on this lofty vaſe's ſide,
Where China's gayeſt art has dy'd
The azure flow'rs that blow;
Demureſt of the tabby kind,
The penſive Selima reclin'd,
Gaz'd on the lake below.

In the winding cloiſters on the right hand are ſome ancient bas-reliefs; and a braſs plate with the effigies of Ralph Walpole biſhop of Norwich and Ely, engraven by Müntz (a Swiſs painter who lived ſome time with Mr. Walpole), and a Chineſe lanthorn with ſcraped oyſter-ſhells.

You

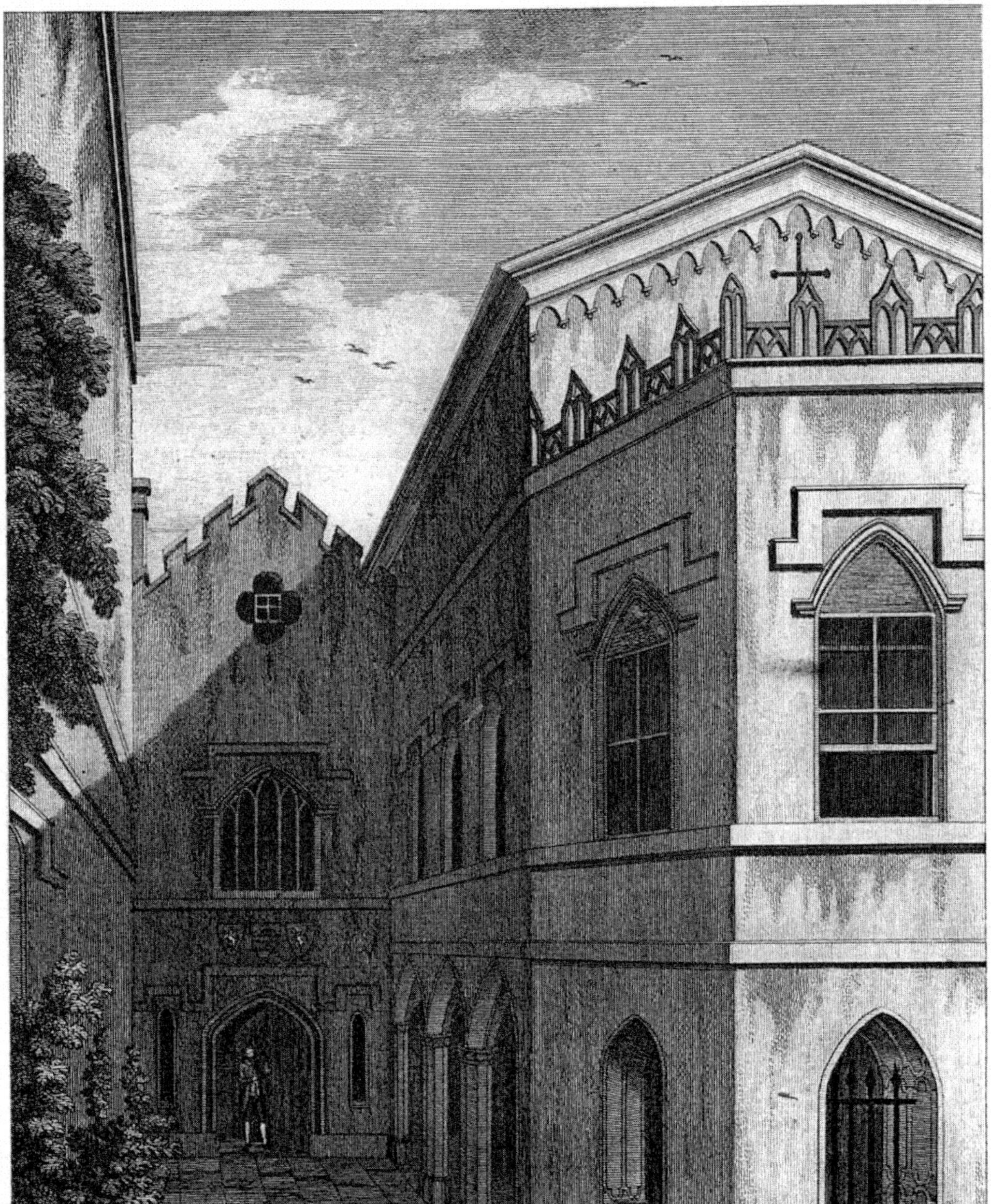

E. Edwards delin. J. Newton sculp.

ENTRANCE of STRAWBERRY HILL.

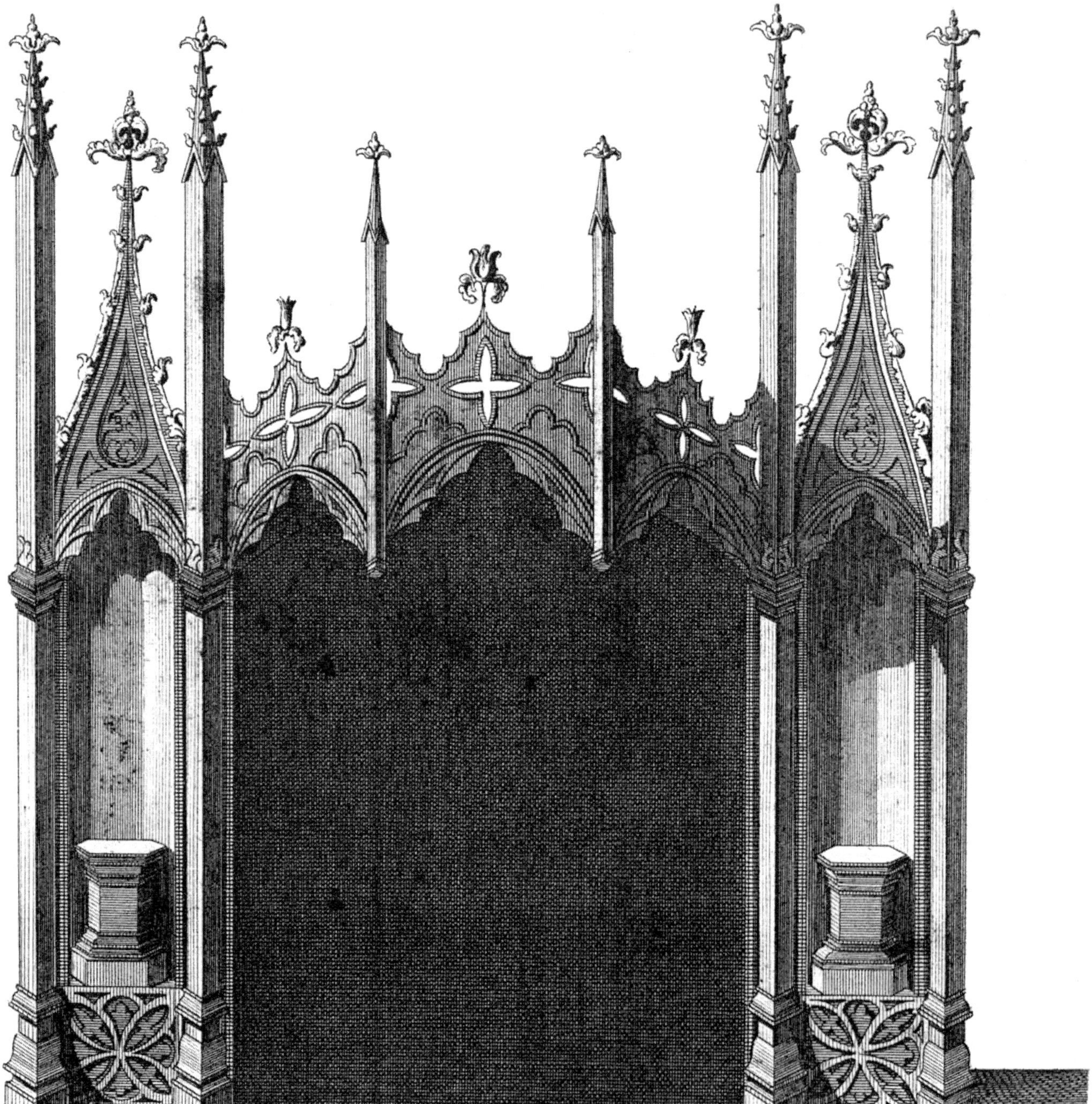

J. Morris sc

CHIMNEY IN THE GREAT PARLOUR.

You firſt enter a ſmall gloomy hall paved with hexagon tiles, and lighted by two narrow windows of painted glaſs, repreſenting St. John and St. Francis. This hall is united with the ſtaircaſe, and both are hung with gothic paper, painted by one Tudor, from the ſcreen of prince Arthur's tomb in the cathedral of Worceſter. The baluſtrade was deſigned by Mr. Bentley; at every corner is an antelope (one of lord Orford's ſupporters) holding a ſhield. In the well of the ſtaircaſe, by a cord of black and yellow, hangs a gothic lanthorn of tin japanned, deſigned by Mr. Bentley, and filled with painted glaſs; the door of it has an old pane with the arms of Vere earl of Oxford.

Turning to the left, through a ſmall paſſage, over the entrance of which is an ancient carving in wood of the arms of queen Elizabeth, 1567, and in it a window of painted glaſs, you enter

THE REFECTORY, OR GREAT PARLOUR.

IT is thirty feet long, twenty wide, and twelve high; hung with paper in imitation of ſtucco. The chimney-piece was deſigned by Mr. Bentley: upon it ſtands a fine Etruſcan vaſe, between two bottles of black and gold porcelaine.

Over the chimney, a converſation, by Reynolds, ſmall life: Richard ſecond lord Edgcumbe is drawing at a table in the library at Strawberry-hill; George James Williams is looking over him; George Auguſtus Selwyn ſtands on the other ſide with a book in his hand. Lord Edgcumbe, Mr. Selwyn and Mr. Williams uſed to be with Mr. Walpole at Chriſtmas and Eaſter at Strawberry-hill.

On one ſide of this picture, a head of ſir Horace Mann, reſident at Florence; painted there by Aſtley, and highly coloured: he is dreſt in red velvet.

Oppoſite to it, his brother Galfridus Mann, in brown; by the ſame.

Over againſt the chimney, a bureau of black japan; on it a clock, ſupported by a bronze figure of a woman reading: beneath, an Etruſcan vaſe, between two white old china beakers.

The chairs are black, of a gothic pattern, defigned by Mr. Bentley and Mr. Walpole. The table of Sicilian jafper on a black frame defigned by Mr. Bentley: upon it, a large punch-bowl and pail of Seve china; two beakers of old grey porcelaine, veined; two ice-pails of Chelfea china. Under it, two Etrufcan vafes, and a jar of Roman fayence. Over the table hangs a hunting-horn, finely enamelled on one fide in colours, on the other in chiaro fcuro, with the hiftory of faint Hubert. By the table an old white china bottle, ornamented with or moulu, on a mahogany pedeftal, for water, bought at Mr. Bateman's fale, 1775.

On each fide of the window, the top of which has fome fine painted glafs, and one ridiculous * Dutch piece reprefenting the triumph of Fame, who is accompanied by Cato, Cicero, and other great men, in fquare caps and gowns of mafters of arts, are card-tables of rofe-wood, carved in China; and over each a looking-glafs in a gothic frame of black and gold, defigned by Mr. Walpole. Inclofed in the tops of the frames, with their arms and coronets, are the portraits of George Walpole third earl of Orford, and of George Cholmondeley vifcount Malpas, eldeft fon of George earl of Cholmondeley and of Mary fecond daughter of fir Robert Walpole. The former is copied by Eckardt, from a miniature by Liotard, in the cabinet above ftairs: the latter is original by Eckardt. On one fide of the window,

An old woman letting a boy light his candle, by Schalken; very fine.

Oppofite, Two boys, a dog and a goat, by Baffan; from Mr. Jennings's collection.

At the end of the room, over againft the window, fir Robert Walpole, knight of the garter, afterwards earl of Orford. On one fide of him,

Catherine, eldeft daughter of John Shorter, of Bybrook in Kent, firft wife of fir Robert Walpole; in white: a copy from fir Godfrey Kneller, by Jarvis. On the other fide,

Maria Skerret (in the drefs of a fhepherdefs), fecond wife of fir Robert; by Jarvis.

* There is another Dutch emblematic pane, on which is Charles II. riding uppermoft on the wheel of Fortune, and Rebellion thrown down. Another pane is painted with a cobler whiftling to a bird in a cage, by Pearfon, fcholar of Price. This window was altered and enlarged in 1774.

On one ſide of the chimney, Robert Walpole ſecond earl of Orford, auditor of the exchequer, maſter of the fox-hounds, and knight of the bath, eldeſt ſon of ſir Robert Walpole by his firſt wife; in red velvet, with a globe by him: by Richardſon.

Margaret, only child of Samuel Rolle of Heynton in Devonſhire, firſt married to Robert ſecond earl of Orford, and mother of George the third earl; and ſecondly to Sewallis Shirley, a younger ſon of earl Ferrers; in a white riding-habit with a ſtick: by Jarvis.

On the other ſide, ſir Edward Walpole, ſecond ſon of ſir Robert Walpole and Catherine Shorter, knight of the bath, and clerk of the pells; in the robes of the bath: by Slaughter.

Horace Walpole, third ſon of ſir Robert and Catherine Shorter; in blue velvet: by Richardſon.

Over againſt the chimney, a large piece of the ladies Laura, Maria, and Horatia Waldegrave, daughters of James ſecond earl of Waldegrave and Maria Walpole, afterwards ducheſs of Glouceſter; by ſir Joſhua Reynolds, 1781.

Lady Anne Oſborn *, daughter of the firſt duke of Leeds; by ſir Godfrey Kneller. She was firſt married to Thomas Coke of Holkam, by whom ſhe was grandmother of Thomas Coke lord Lovel and earl of Leiceſter; and ſecondly to Horatio Walpole, ſecond ſon of ſir Edward Walpole, and uncle of ſir Robert Walpole. On the other ſide,

Dorothy, ſiſter of ſir Robert, and ſecond wife of Charles lord viſcount Townſhend, knight of the garter and ſecretary of ſtate; in a Turkiſh habit: by Jarvis.

Over one of the doors, Mary lady Malpas, ſecond daughter of ſir Robert Walpole and Catherine Shorter; married to George lord Malpas, afterwards earl of Cholmondeley: by Eckardt, after Jarvis. Over the other door,

Lady Maria Walpole, only child of ſir Robert Walpole and Maria Sker-

* This is a whole length picture, but is turned in.

ret, and wife of Charles Churchill, only ſon of general Churchill; in a veil, with a muſic-book before her: by Eckardt.

A fire-ſcreen of admirable needle-work, repreſenting a vaſe of flowers, by lady Caroline Campbell, daughter of John duke of Argyll, counteſs of Aileſbury; married ſecondly to general Henry Seymour Conway, only brother of Francis firſt earl of Hertford of that line, knight of the garter, embaſſador in France, and lord chamberlain: it is mounted in mahogany, carved, and inlaid with ivory.

A Turkey carpet, and a fire-ſcreen embroidered with knotting.

A two-leafed ſcreen, containing part of a map of Surry and Middleſex. It is a piece of the firſt tapeſtry woven in England, and came from Weſton in Warwickſhire, the ſeat of the Sheldons, who introduced the manufacture. The complete ſuite of hangings were purchaſed by Mr. Walpole, and preſented by him to the earl of Harcourt. This ſpecimen had never been hung up.

IN THE WAITING-ROOM.

A HEAD in artificial ſtone of John Dryden the poet, great uncle of Catherine Shorter lady Walpole: a large altar candleſtick of metal, inlaid with gothic inſcriptions, very ancient: and a pair of ancient bellows.

Inſide of King's college chapel, by Canaletti.

A curious emblematic picture of a man ſtanding, ſmall whole length, with a buſt of Charles II. ſeemingly before his reſtoration, for a cupid is weighing the broken arms of England (as a commonwealth) againſt crowns and ſceptres, (but the ſceptre is a French one, and therefore probably painted abroad) fragments of architecture, and the man holds a plan like St. Paul's; thence it has been ſuppoſed a portrait of ſir Chriſtopher Wren, but does not reſemble him, nor are the arms his.

A print of lady Mary Coke.

Buſt of Colley Cibber, poet-laureat, in a cap, when old, coloured from the life, and extremely like. He gave it to Mrs. Clive, the celebrated actreſs; and her brother Mr. Raſtor gave it, after her death, to Mr. Walpole.

Tradeſcant

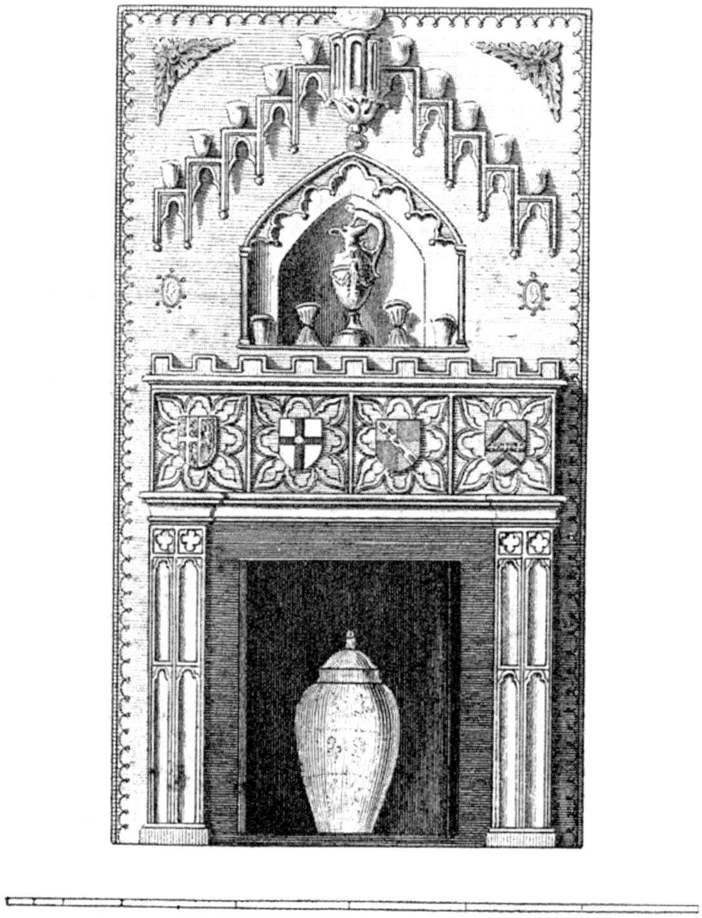

CHIMNEY IN THE CHINA ROOM.

Tradeſcant junior, with a ſkull covered with moſs for the powder of ſympathy.

A ſmall whole length of Dryden, in oil, by Maubert.

THE CHINA-ROOM.

PAINTED glaſs in the windows, and creſts of Shorter and Geſtinthorpe: the ceiling painted with convolvuluses on poles, by Müntz, from a ceiling in the little Borgheſe villa at Freſcati: the ſides, white Dutch tiles, with borders of blue and white.

In the floor ſome very ancient tiles with arms, from the cathedral at Glouceſter. The upper part of the chimney-piece is taken from a window of an ancient farm-houſe, formerly Bradfield-hall, belonging to lord Grimſton in Eſſex; the lower part from a chimney at Hurſt Monceaux in Suſſex: it is adorned with the arms of Talbot, Bridges, Sackville, and Walpole, the principal perſons who have inhabited Strawberry-hill.

In a niche ſupported by two columns of oriental alabaſter, over the chimney, is a fine ewer of fayence, deſigned by Julio Romano; and two green glaſs tumblers, with golden edges; and two round ſaltcellars of old blue and gold Venetian glaſs, with flowers.

Over the niche, four chocolate cups of fayence, by Pietro Cortona; and a bronze medallion of Pandulfo Malateſta.

On the ſides, George II. and Frederic prince of Wales, in Batterſea enamel.

In the chimney, a large jar of old blue and white china; and two tiles from Byſham-abbey.

On the ſhelves and floor is a collection of porcelaine, earthenware, glaſs, and enamel on copper, of various ages and countries, as follow:

Two dozen plates of Venetian glaſs; each plate has a different view of Venice, drawn in red.

A japanned tray with a vaſe for cream, and eight chocolate-cups and ſaucers with landſcapes in brown, of the ſame ware.

 Two

Two bowls of Worcefter porcelaine, the pattern from old china.

Two muftard-pots and plates, of Seve china; given by lord Hertford.

Five trays, in fhapes of fans, of old Japan china.

An old blue and white plate with a rib in the middle.

A coloured handle cup, faucer and fquare plate, à la Grecque, of Seve china.

Two old blue and white plates, artichoke pattern.

Thirteen ditto, with peacock feathers.

Sixteen coloured old Japan plates.

Four ditto, blue and white, with figures.

Three ditto, with figures.

Twelve ditto, of coloured Japan china.

Four ditto, with birds.

Four water-plates with figures, of new china.

Twelve plates of Chelfea china, with fmall coloured birds.

Three difhes fcolloped and ribbed, with coloured flowers.

Two large coloured difhes of the fine old thick Japan china.

A large deep difh of Roman earth, with ftories from Ovid's Metamorphofis.

An earthen-ware difh, with the heads of Charles II. and queen Catherine in blue and white; a prefent from Mr. Ibbot.

An old blue and white difh, with landfcapes.

Ditto, larger, with figures.

Two difhes of very old French earthen-ware, with the arms of France.

Two fmall difhes of fayence, with grotefques, and the arms of a bifhop Contarini.

An

An octagon coloured plate of Saxon china, old pattern.

An octagon square plate, with a cock and hen.

A dish and twelve plates enamelled on copper.

Two round plates of Japan.

Thirteen old white chocolate cups and tea-cups, with embossed flowers.

A tea-pot, milk-pot, five coffee-cups, five tea-cups, and ten saucers, of white quilted china of St. Cloud.

A tea-pot and milk-pot, six cups and saucers, of modern china, with grey landscapes.

Five white cups and saucers with gold borders.

Two coloured caudle-cups.

An earthen-ware tea-pot, with the head of lord Chatham.

A small tea-canister of Seve china, blue and gold, with figures on white.

A pot pourri of Saxon china, with coloured flowers embossed.

An old white china cup, with cupids painted in Europe.

A cup with a bullfinch, of modern china.

Thirteen small baskets of Saxon china for sugar-plums, different patterns.

An urn and stand of kennel coal, a present from sir William Meredith.

Six coloured water-cups and plates of Chelsea china.

A blue and white caudle-cup.

Two ditto, coloured.

An old blue and white honeycomb tea-pot.

Two Roman lacrymatories of glass, two of earth, and two water-glasses. M.

An ewer enamelled with bacchanals on copper.

Two coffee-cups and ſaucers of white and gold Bohemian glaſs.

A cup of Mr. Place's china. *Vide Walpole's Catalogue of Engliſh Engravers.*

A blue and white ſaucer, with a landſcape, of fine Nankin china.

A jar, with red and white landſcapes and blue and gold borders, of Chelſea china.

Two coloured Saxon trays, with ſquirrels.

A ſcolloped ſaucer of Saxon china, the ſecond ſort, very rare: in it lies a medal of Louis quinze in Seve china.

A hand-candleſtick of coloured Seve china.

A blue and gold ſugar-diſh of old Venetian glaſs, cover and plate, with a ſilver gilt ſpoon.

An old blue and white ſaucer in the ſhape of a ſtar.

Two trays, ditto.

An ivory drinking-horn, with the arms of the earls of Exeter; ancient.

An old earthen mug of Arabian ware.

Two vaſes with handles, of red Portugueſe earth.

Two plates like ſhaving-baſons, of the ſame.

An earthen bottle; painted on it, *Sack*, 1647: it was thus ſold by apothecaries. From the collection of Mrs. Kennon, the virtuoſa midwife.

A blue and white eggſhell cup.

Michael Angelo's Bacchus, made in the china of the comte de Lauragais; from the collection of the comte de Caylus.

Two Roman glaſſes, like water-glaſſes; two lacrymatories, ditto; and two of earth. M.

Buſt of Voltaire, in biſcuit of Nancy.

Two

Two blue and gold cups for eggs, of Seve china.

Seven old coloured octagon cups and ſaucers.

A tea-pot and baſon, ſix handle cups and ſaucers, with battles in black, of Vienna china; a preſent to Catherine lady Walpole from count Dehn, envoy from the duke of Wolfenbuttle.

A ſquare brown china cup to meaſure tea.

An old white china tea-pot with birds and flowers finely painted in Europe.

A bagpiping boy and a dancing girl, of Seve biſcuit.

Six fine old cups, white within; without, japanned black and mother of pearl: very rare.

An ewer enamelled on copper, with naked horſemen fighting.

A blue and gold coffee-cup and ſaucer, with birds on white cartouches, of Seve china.

A cup and ſaucer, all blue and gold, of ditto.

An old glaſs tankard, with a battle of Turks and Chriſtians in black, finely drawn.

Ditto of old Venetian glaſs ſtriped with white, mounted in ſilver gilt: on the lid, arms of Parr enamelled.

Six handle cups and ſaucers with green landſcapes on white, of Chelſea china.

An urn and cover of red Portugueſe earth.

Two large coloured ſaucers with figures.

Two ſmall ditto baſons with flowers.

Two large coloured baſons.

Two white ſaltcellars with crawfiſh in relief, of Chelſea china.

A fine ſquare plate, à la Grecque, of Seve china.

Two old blue and white trays.

Two Saxon coloured ſaucers, cinquefoil.

Two green and gold ſalts, with flowers on white, of Seve china.

Two white Chelſea ſalts on feet.

Two ſmall blue and white baſons.

A boy ſupporting a ſhell, finely modelled in red earth; the firſt ſort of Saxon china before it was glazed or painted, and which was only given as preſents by the elector: extremely rare.

Three pieces of rocks, made of rice; given by Mr. Raftor, Mrs. Clive's brother.

Two Chineſe baſons enamelled with coloured flowers on copper.

A red cup and ſaucer, glazed; the ſecond ſort of Saxon china: rare.

Two blue and gold handle cups and ſaucers, with birds on white cartouches, of Seve china.

One ditto, green.

One ditto, blue and gold in zigzags, and garlands on white; very beautiful.

Two white barrels with vines and grapes, of Chelſea china.

Two ſmall baſons with coloured flowers, of the beſt modern china.

A very fine ſtanding cup and cover, enamelled on copper with the ſtory of Sampſon, from the deſigns of Parmegiano.

A ſmall dejeuné of blue and gold Seve china; very pretty.

A handle cup, ſaucer, and ſquare plate, of blue and gold Seve china, with ſea-pieces admirably copied from Vernet's pictures.

Ditto of blue, green, and gold, with flowers on white.

Two porringers of Portugueſe earth.

An octagon ſaltcellar enamelled on copper, droll figures on the ſides with old French verſes; at top, a head, *Je ſuis Paris*; at bottom, another, *La belle Helene*.

A copper tray, ſcolloped and enamelled with ſaint John and flowers; a preſent from Mr. G. Montagu.

A very large glaſs urn, damaged, found near London; a preſent from Dr. Ch. Lyttelton biſhop of Carliſle.

Six coloured handle cups and ſaucers, a tea-pot and ſugar-diſh, in ſhapes of leaves, of Chantilli china.

Four ſmall blue and white eggſhell cups.

The preſent queen of France, a large medallion of Seve biſcuit; a preſent from the ducheſs dowager d'Aiguillon in 1771.

Two handle cups and ſaucers, different patterns à la Grecque, of Seve china.

Two butter-pots and plates of blue and white Delft ware; preſents from lady Aileſbury.

A red cup and ſaucer, clouded.

A ſmall ſquare brown tea-pot.

A jug of old clouded glaſs, and a bottle of the ſame.

Two Saxon tankards, one with Chineſe figures, the other with European. Theſe tankards are extremely remarkable. Sir Robert Walpole drank ale; the ducheſs of Kendal, miſtreſs of king George the firſt, gave him the former. A dozen or more years afterwards, the counteſs of Yarmouth, miſtreſs of king George the ſecond, without having ſeen the other, gave him the ſecond; and they match exactly in form and ſize.

Two deſſert-diſhes of coloured Japan china.

A ſcolloped ſugar-diſh of old china, white without, ſtriped with colours within: rare.

A baſon and plate of ſcolloped Saxon china.

A plate with ſmall flowers, ditto.

 A monteith

A monteith of coloured Seve china: beautiful.

Two old white china candlesticks, mounted in silver.

A large scolloped and coloured bowl of Japan china.

A pale green and white flat bason; very old.

Two green jars.

A mug of earthen ware, with Arabic characters.

A sugar-dish, cover and plate, of Japan china.

A green ewer with a purple handle.

An Etruscan cup with two handles, and an owl on it.

Two very small brown tea-pots.

Medallion of Henry quatre, in Seve biscuit.

Four blue and white chocolate cups, and four saucers.

A triangular saltcellar of fayence, with fine figures on terms.

An old Venetian glass cup and saucer, with gold flowers.

A cup of Matlock spar, on a foot.

An urn, ditto.

Four dessert-plates of fayence, with figures and boys round the borders; by Pietro Cortona: very fine. A fifth ditto, with goats; a present from lady Diana Beauclerc.

Two light purple handle cups and saucers with landscapes, of Seve china.

A larger cup and saucer, à la Grecque, ditto.

A scolloped japan tray.

A fine glass urn with golden boys; Roman: described in doctor Middleton's Antiquities.

A tall blue and white tea-pot with flat sides.

A round brown tea-pot, quite flat.

A fine old blue and white box and cover, a present from lady Ailesbury.

A vase with two handles, of Portuguese earth.

A cup, ditto, with fantastic forms within it: given by lady Mary Churchill.

A green and white mug and saucer, with figures on white, of Seve china.

Ditto with rustic implements; very genteel.

A white old triangular piece of china and cover, for eggs.

An old white beaker.

Two large blue and white tea-pots.

Twelve old blue and white dessert-plates with figures.

A small dish of Chelsea china in a dessert pattern.

A blue and white beaker with a Chinese procession.

Two blue and white soup-dishes with figures.

Ten dishes of old Japan ware.

An ancient tall drinking-glass, with arms and devices; a present from sir John Hawkins.

Two large blue and white beakers.

Two ditto, of different patterns: a companion to one of them is in the great bedchamber.

A blue and white dish of Chelsea china.

A Turkish earthen bottle, with leaves cast in relief on it.

Two blue and white jars.

Two green, blue, and white beakers.

Two blue and white beakers.

A large

A large fayence diſh.

A fine Turkiſh jar and cover, with caſt leaves: curious.

A large blue and white diſh.

A blue and white baſket of Chantilli china.

A white Seve ſaucepan that bears the fire: 1771.

Two blue and white beakers.

Two ſmall coloured ditto.

Two ſquare blue and white bottles.

An odd green and white tea-pot.

A tile from the kitchen of William the Conqueror at Caen in Normandy.

Two baſons of moſt ancient Gombroon china; a preſent from lord Vere, out of the collection of lady Elizabeth Germaine.

A beautiful green baſon.

Ten coloured pattypans of different ſizes.

An old white diſh.

A diſh and four deſſert-plates, brown, blue, and white.

A large blue and white diſh, and a ſmall ditto.

Four green leaves of Staffordſhire-ware for a deſſert.

A tea-kettle of brown china.

A white jar.

Two white handle cups and ſaucers, finely painted with natural flowers, of Seve porcelaine.

A Mercury, ditto.

A group

A group of the graces supporting a basket, of Seve biscuit.

A large old white china tea-pot, that was the duke of Monmouth's; a present from Simon second earl of Harcourt.

A sauce-boat of Roman fayence, with Cupid riding on a dolphin.

Twelve plates of Wedgwood's ware, with cameos of blue and white, and blue festoons; from a design of lady Diana Beauclerc.

A bason and ewer of Roman fayence, painted with landscapes; a present from the earl of Exeter.

A large round vase and cover, and a dish to it, of Roman fayence.

Two dishes of the same.

A cup and saucer, white, with green festoons, of Bristol porcelaine.

A round picture of white flowers in alto relievo, of the same manufacture.

A square compotier with blue and gold flowers, of Salopian porcelaine.

A blue, gold, and coloured sugar-dish and plate, of Worcester porcelaine.

Two white glass cups, with gold festoons and rams' heads, of English manufacture.

Two dessert-plates of old china, in form of herons.

A group of two figures and five single cupids, of Hesse and Brunswick porcelaine; presents from lord Beauchamp.

Sir William Hamilton, envoy at Naples, and Catherine lady Walpole; medallions of Wedgwood's ware.

Louis quinze, and Dr. Franklin, medallions in biscuit.

Two tall chocolate cups and saucers, beautifully painted with holyoaks, of Seve china; presents from lady Ailesbury.

A white and gold mug and saucer, with Chinese pheasants, of ditto.

A cup and saucer of ditto, all over strawberries, a present from madame du Deffand.

A cup

A cup and ſaucer of ditto, lilac and gold, with the ſtory of Pan and Syrinx in crimſon.

A cup and ſaucer of Wedgwood's ware, finely painted with Engliſh views.

A white and gold handle cup and ſaucer with Chineſe figures, of the porcelaine of Clignancour, a new manufacture eſtabliſhed by the comte de Provence, called porcelaine de Monſieur.

A cup to hold an egg, imitating lapis lazuli; porcelaine de Seve.

A very ſmall cup and ſaucer, white and gold, with imitations of rubies; ditto.

A large caudle cup, ſtriped with gold, and flowers; porcelaine of Berlin.

Four ditto, with ſprigs of flowers on white ground; ditto.

A tea-pot and plate, baſon, ſugar-diſh, milk-pot, two chocolate-cups, two pomatum-pots, and a cann, ; of the Staffordſhire bamboo ware, 1782.

A Turkiſh earthen-ware plate, brown and gold, a preſent from Mrs. Griffith the authoreſs.

A white glaſs ſugar-diſh, painted with natural flowers.

A red Portugueſe bowl with a grate at the bottom, for cooling water.

Three black and red earthen vaſes, with handles, highly poliſhed.

Two more copper enamelled plates, given by lady Aileſbury.

A tumbler, of crackled china within; japanned without; very rare: a preſent from Mrs. French.

A baſon of Turkiſh earthen-ware, gilt within; a preſent from Mr. Fitzwilliam.

A glaſs ſaucer, gilt and ſilvered; given by lord Oſſory.

Portrait of George Simon earl of Harcourt, in Wedgwood's ware; the only one executed in that manner.

A Tuſcan vaſe of Wedgwood's ware.

A white

A white cup and ſaucer with coloured flowers, made for the comte d'Artois, and called porcelaine d'Angouleme; a preſent from the viſcounteſs Mount-Edgcumbe.

Two cuſtard cups of old crackled china, with flowers of plated ſilver.

A ſmall jar, white within and japanned without; a preſent from Mr. Barrett of Lee.

A Delft beaker, and two blue and white bottles, ditto.

A large flattiſh drinking glaſs, one of the firſt manufacture at Venice, with the initials of an Engliſh lady's name for whom it was made, and the date 1580; a preſent from lady Georgina Smythe.

Three pieces of Mooriſh moſaic; on one a ſhield, with the name or title of a Mooriſh king; bought at the auction of Mr. Carter, who publiſhed an account of Spain.

Two vaſes of white porcelaine, ſtriped with blue and gold, and ornamented with red feſtoons; from the manufacture of marquis Ginori at Florence: ſent by ſir Horace Mann.

China in the Waiting-Room.

Two ice-pails with vines, of Saxon china.

A white butter-pot and plate of Chantilli, and two blue and white ſalt-cellars, ditto.

Two monteiths of Tolle, a new French metal japanned.

Four oblong deſſert-diſhes, four leaves, and twelve plates, with coloured fruits and flowers, of Chelſea china.

Twelve blue and white coffee-cups and ſaucers of Chantilli.

Twelve black and white tea-cups and ſaucers of Bow china.

Two red and white handle cups and ſaucers with boys, of Seve.

A fine coloured ice-pail and cover, ditto.

A blue and white Delft butter-pot and plate.

Two white and gold ſalts of Seve.

Twenty-four white plates with knurled borders and gold edges, four deep leaves, two ſquare plates, and a cream bowl, of Seve.

A large white plate, and a white glaſs beaker.

A blue and white baſket, two round cheeſe-pots and plate, and a ſceau for liquors, of Chantilli.

Twelve fine plates coloured, with rich blue edges, of Seve.

Two ditto, larger.

Six ditto, blue and white.

Two green Staffordſhire flower-pots with maſks, and two plates.

The LITTLE PARLOUR.

OVER the door is a ſhield of Mr. Walpole's arms and quarterings on painted glaſs, by Price. The room is lighted by a bow window, in which, among other pieces of painted glaſs, are the arms of Ayliffe, impaling Clifford of Frampton: given by Mr. George Selwyn.

The chimney is taken from the tomb of Thomas Ruthall biſhop of Durham, in Weſtminſter-abbey. The room is hung with gothic paper of ſtone colour in moſaic, on which are wooden prints by Jackſon of Venice; and furniſhed with a table and eight chairs of ebony, bought at the lady Conyers's at Great Stoughton in Huntingdonſhire, as were others in other chambers. On the table is an ice-pail of Wedgwood's ware.

Two ſleeping dogs, the original model in terra-cotta, by the honourable Mrs. Damer, which ſhe afterwards executed in marble for the duke of Richmond.

In the YELLOW BEDCHAMBER, or BEAUTY-ROOM.

THE chimney-piece was deſigned by Mr. Bentley. The room is hung with grey ſpotted paper, the bed and chairs of yellow ſilk and ſtuff damaſk. On the ebony table, two large old blue and white china candle-

CHIMNEY IN THE YELLOW BED CHAMBER.

ſticks, and a writing-box of ſandal-wood inlaid with ivory. On the commode with a ſlab of white marble, bought at Mr. Bateman's ſale, a bronze caſt of the Hermaphrodite. A fire-ſcreen worked by lady Oſſory, 1781.

Over the chimney, Charles II, James duke of York and Mary princeſs of Orange, when children, copied from Vandyck by Charles Beale.

A fine portrait of ſir Peter Lely, after himſelf, by ditto.

Elizabeth Wriotheſly counteſs of Southampton, and afterwards firſt wife of Ralph the firſt duke of Montagu, by ditto, after ditto. Theſe three are in water-colours.

Nineteen ſmall heads, in oil, of the court of Charles II. (except Sachariſſa) copied by Jarvis for himſelf, and bought with his houſe at Hampton by Mr. Lovibonde, at whoſe ſale theſe and the three foregoing were purchaſed.

Charles the ſecond.

Queen Catherine.

King William, when prince of Orange.

Queen Mary, when princeſs.

Catharine Sidley, counteſs of Dorcheſter, miſtreſs of James II.

Frances Stuart (of Grammont's Memoires) ducheſs of Richmond.

Louiſe de Querouaille, ducheſs of Portſmouth.

Lady Dorothy Sidney, counteſs of Sunderland, Waller's Sachariſſa.

Barbara Villiers, ducheſs of Cleveland.

Arabella Churchill, wife of Mr. Godfrey, miſtreſs of James II.

Mrs. Philadelphia Saunders.

Mrs. Trevor, maid of honour: having ſeen the duke of Monmouth in bed with another lady, and divulged it, the duke engaged Mr. Thynne to debauch her. Mr. Thynne being killed before he bedded lady Ogle, this epigram was made on him:

Here lies Tom Thynne of Longleat-hall,
Who never would have miſcarried,
Had he married the woman he lay withal,
Or lain with the woman he married.

Lady Anne Cavendiſh, daughter of William earl of Devonſhire, and wife of John earl of Exeter.

Lady Gertrude Pierpoint, daughter of William earl of Kingſton, and wife of George Saville marquis of Halifax.

Lady Mary Rich, daughter of Robert earl of Warwick, wife of Henry viſcount St. John, and mother of the famous lord Bolingbroke.

Henry earl of Ogle, only ſon of Henry Cavendiſh duke of Newcaſtle.

Lady Elizabeth Percy, only daughter and heireſs of Joceline laſt earl of Northumberland, married firſt to Henry lord Ogle, ſecondly to Thomas Thynne, eſq. and laſtly to Charles Seymour duke of Somerſet.

Two other ladies, unknown.

Over the door, Mary queen of Scots, by Vertue.

Lady Anne Hamilton, daughter of W. duke of Hamilton, and wife of Robert Carnegie earl of Southeſk.

Lady Elizabeth Butler, daughter of James duke of Ormond, and wife of Philip Stanhope earl of Cheſterfield. Theſe two heads are copied in chalks by Mr. Farringdon, from the originals by ſir Peter Lely, at Mr. Fountaine's at Narford. *See an account of the two ladies in the Memoires de Grammont.*

Buſt of the lady viſcounteſs Melbourne; a caſt from the original by Mrs. Damer.

Prince Arthur and Catharine of Arragon, on board, in the original frame; a preſent from colonel Myddelton of Denbighſhire, in which county it had remained from the death of the prince at Ludlow.

On the Stair-Case.

View of Richmond-hill, the original drawing by Mr. Henry Bunbury; a preſent from himſelf.

THE

THE BREAKFAST-ROOM, ONE PAIR OF STAIRS.

FURNISHED with blue paper, and blue and white linen. Black and yellow painted glaſs ſet in plain blue glaſs in the bow window. On the writing-table, an inlaid writing-box made by Langlois. The chimney-piece and windows are not truly gothic, but were deſigned by Mr. W. Robinſon of the Board of Works, before there was any deſign of farther improvements to the houſe.

Over the chimney, a glaſs in an ebony frame, a preſent from the reverend Mr. Hemmings of Twickenham; two blue and white flower-pots of Seve china; and two candleſticks with Chineſe figures, by Martin, and china flowers. On one ſide of the glaſs,

Mary Lepelle lady Hervey; a print.

A moonlight; by Bernard Lens.

A frame with nine miniatures, viz.

A young bride, by Iſaac Oliver.

A lady; behind her a red curtain. Both of the family of Digby, but not known.

Venetia Stanley lady Digby, aged nineteen, very beautiful; by Peter Oliver.

Sir Kenelm Digby and lady Digby, after Vandyck; by ditto: ſet in the form of a book with covers of gold enamelled.

The ſame lady Digby, as ſhe was found dead in her bed; by ditto, after ditto; ſet in gold enamelled black; on which behind is a ſphere: it ſeems to mean, that the world was in mourning for her. Sir Kenelm was paſſionately fond of this lady, who, lord Clarendon ſays, was of *extraordinary beauty and as extraordinary fame*. At Windſor is a whole length of her, by Vandyck, treading on ſerpents, to imply that the ſtories told of her were the produce of malice. At Goathurſt, where they lived, are two buſts of her in bronze; on the pedeſtal of one are inſcribed theſe tender words, *Uxorem vivam amare voluptas, defunctam religio.*

Sir

Sir Kenelm Digby, when young; by Peter Oliver: very fine.

Lady Digby, again, moſt beautiful; by ditto.

Lady Lucy Percy, daughter and coheireſs of Thomas earl of Northumberland who was beheaded, wife of ſir Edward Stanley, younger ſon of the earl of Derby, mother of Venetia lady Digby; by Iſaac Oliver. She is ſtill more beautiful than her daughter, though dreſt very unbecomingly in a great black hat and large ruff; only ſet off by a lilac ground. This is perhaps the fineſt and moſt perfect miniature in the world. All the ſeven laſt are wonderfully preſerved, though found in a garret in an old houſe in Wales, belonging to a Mr. Watkin Williams, probably deſcended from ſir Kenelm, one of whoſe ſons left only two daughters, that were married into Welch families. This ſet of pictures, with a few more leſs fine, coſt Mr. Walpole 300 guineas.

On the other ſide of the glaſs, another frame, with fifteen miniatures, viz. Robert earl of Eſſex, favourite of queen Elizabeth; ſet in a caſe enamelled with flowers.

Henry Carey lord Hunſdon, knight of the garter 1585; by Hilliard: ſet in black enamel. Theſe two from the collection of lady Elizabeth Germaine.

A lady of the family of Digby; belonging to the ſet above-named; in a white enamelled caſe.

The duc de Vendome, with a red knot; by Petitot.

Madame la princeſſe Palatine; by ditto.

Madame la ducheſſe de Montpenſier, grandmother of Mademoiſelle; by ditto. Theſe three from the collection of the comte de Caylus.

La ducheſſe de Montzabon, called La Belle des Belles; by ditto.

Holbein, in a round, original by himſelf.

An exceedingly fine watch, given to general Fairfax by the parliament after the battle of Naſeby; by P. Bordier, brother-in-law of Petitot. On one ſide is Fairfax on horſeback, after Vandyck's king Charles; on the other,

other, the houſe of commons; behind, the battle. It was bought at the ſale of Thoreſby's muſeum, who has deſcribed it in his Ducatus Leodienſis.

Two boys, ſons of ſir Kenelm Digby. Note, theſe and ſome after-mentioned pictures of the Digbys were the other diviſion of that collection, and were purchaſed by Mr. W. of the lady who ſhared them with the other heir.

John duke of Lauderdale, copied by lady Lucan from the original by Cooper, in the poſſeſſion of lady Greenwich.

William Henry duke of Glouceſter, by lady Lucan after Meyer.

Charlotte de la Tremouille counteſs of Derby; in a frame of ſilver filigrane.

A lady's head, ſuppoſed to be the counteſs of Pembroke, wife of earl William, by Hoſkins; finely preſerved: a preſent from the ducheſs dowager of Portland.

Fontenelle, a drawing; bequeathed to Mr. Walpole by lady Hervey.

A landſcape, a drawing in water-colours, by Vanderneer.

Inſide of Walpole church in Lincolnſhire; by Vertue.

View of Mad. du Deffand's room and cats, a print; with verſes by the preſident Henault.

A print of count Antoine Hamilton.

A moſt curious picture of Roſe the royal gardener, preſenting the firſt pine-apple raiſed in England to Charles II. who is ſtanding in a garden: the houſe ſeems to be Dawny-court near Windſor, the villa of the ducheſs of Cleveland. The whole piece is well painted, probably by Danckers. It was a preſent to Mr. W. from the rev. Mr. Pennicott of Ditton, to whom it was bequeathed by Mr. London, grandſon of him who was partner with Wiſe.

Two prints of Rubens's own houſe.

Two beautiful bas-reliefs of boys in wax, by lady Diana Beauclerc; ſet in frames with her arms, and cameos by Wedgwood and Taſſie.

Van-

Vandervaart the painter, by himſelf, in water-colours, finely done; in an old ebony frame ſet with lapis lazuli and agates: a preſent from Richard Bull, eſq.

Cowley, by ſir Peter Lely; the fine original of Zincke's Cowley in enamel in the cabinet; bought at the ſale of Mr. Lovibonde in 1776*.

Two views of Paris, by Raguenet; given by Henry Fox lord Holland.

Four waſhed views of the chateau de Grignan in Provence: a preſent from George Hardinge, eſq.

Miſs Temple, maid of honour to Anne Hyde ducheſs of York, and ſecond wife of ſir Charles Lyttelton; by Spenſer, after the unfiniſhed picture by Cooper, in the poſſeſſion of lord Lyttelton.

Head of the comte de Grammont; copied from the original at the convent of the Grands Auguſtins at Paris.

A ſecretaire of inlaid woods.

Cupid, in Seve china.

Two blue and white ſquare tubs, of ditto.

* Deſcription of a young ſhepherd, from Britain's Ida, that almoſt exactly delineates this portrait.

Amongſt the reſt, that all the reſt excell'd,
A daintie boy there wonn'd, whoſe harmleſs yeares
Now in their freſheſt budding gentlie ſwell'd;
His nymph-like face ne'er felt the nimble ſheeres;
Youth's downie bloſſome thro' his cheeke appeares;
His lovelie limbs, but love he quite diſcarded,
Were made for play, but he no play regarded,
And fitt love to reward, and be by love rewarded.

High was his forehead, arch'd with ſilver mould,
Where never anger churliſh wrinkle dighted;
His auburn locks hung like dark threads of gold,
That wanton airs (with their fair length incited)
To play among their wanton curls delighted.
His ſmiling eyes with ſimple truth were ſtor'd——
Ah! how ſhould truth in thoſe thief eyes be ſtor'd,
Which thouſand Loves had ſtol'n, and never once reſtor'd!

Vide Wharton's Obſervations on the Fairy Queen, vol. i. p. 123.

Anne Liddel countess of Ossory; in crayons, by Hamilton.

An urn of granite, brought from one of the Greek islands, and given to sir Robert Walpole by sir Charles Wager.

Ditto of oriental alabaster, given to sir Robert Walpole by general Charles Churchill.

Margaret Smith, wife of sir Charles Bingham lord Lucan; by Hamilton. This lady arrived in five months, by copying in water-colours the enamels and miniatures in this collection, at great perfection, and in that short time copied forty pieces, imitating most exactly the manners of the several masters. Mr. W. wrote the following lines on that subject:

Without a rival, long on painting's throne
Urbino's modest artist sat alone.
At last a British fair's unerring eyes
In five short moons contest the glorious prize.
Raphael by genius, nurs'd by labour, gain'd it—
Bingham but saw perfection, and attain'd it.

Lady Elizabeth Berkeley, wife of lord Craven; by Romney.

Richard III. and his queen; a drawing from painted glass, by Vertue.

A sea-piece; by Backhuysen: very good.

Madame la marquise du Deffand, and the duchesse de Choiseul giving her a doll, which the former, who was blind, holds out her hands to receive; alluding to her calling the duchesse *Grand Maman*. Every part of the room is exactly represented, and madame du Deffand most exactly like, which the duchesse is not; by M. Carmontel, a gentleman belonging to the duke of Orleans, who has done in the same manner most of the court of France: a washed drawing.

A print by Bartolozzi of Georgina Spencer duchess of Devonshire, from the drawing of lady Diana Beauclerc; in a frame with Wedgwood's cameos, and two flies engraved and painted by Hill.

A view of the church of Stokepogeys in Buckinghamshire; the moon shining on Mr. Gray's tomb in the church-yard; by Baron: a present from sir Edward Walpole.

Virgin and child, a highly finished illumination: it belonged to Gaston duke of Orleans.

Francis I. receiving the homage of the clergy, law and army; an illumination; cardinal du Prat as chancellor is at the head of the law. Two of the officers on the fore ground are engraved in Montfaucon's Antiquities of France.

An allegoric washed drawing of Christina of Pisa writing her Cité des Dames, from an illumination in the library of the king of France.

View of the hotel de Carnavalet, where madame de Sevigné lived, in la rue Coulture St. Catherine, at Paris; built by Du Cerceau; painted by Raguenet.

A woman reading; small whole figure; great nature, by Le Duc.

A flower, in paper mosaic, executed by Mrs. Delany, the inventress, who between the seventieth and eightieth years of her age executed 500 plants in this manner. She was daughter of Mr. Granville by the daughter of sir John Stanley, and was first married to Mr. Pendarvis, and then to Dr. Delany.

Its companion, by Mrs. Delany's scholar, miss Jennings of Shiplake.

Lady D. Beauclerc's two daughters, engraved from her drawing by Bartolozzi; in a blue and gold frame painted in mosaic with lions and flower-de-luces, in allusion to the arms of Beauclerc.

Sir Kenelm Digby, his wife and two sons, by Peter Oliver, after Vandyck; a large miniature in the highest preservation; in an ebony case set with Wedgwood's cameos. On the insides of the doors, two other ladies of the same set.

Two other ebony cases, ditto. In one, a lady of the Digby family, half-length, after Vandyck, with a beautiful landscape, by Peter Oliver.

In the other case, lady Digby enamelled, in a frame of the same, with her arms, and Latin mottoes, supported by two goddesses; by G. Toulin, 1637.

Lady Catherine Howard, daughter of H. Fred. earl of Arundel, and first wife of John Digby son of sir Kenelm.

On the reverse, in the same enamelled frame, another lady of the family, exquisitely painted by Peter Oliver; probably the second wife of John Digby.

Lady Frances Howard, countess of Essex and then of Somerset; copied by lady Bingham, now lady Lucan, from the original at Woburn.

Catherine duchess of Buckingham, daughter of James II. in enamel by Zincke: a present from her niece madame de Bouzols.

A holy

A holy family in wax, from Carlo Maratti, by Mrs. Mary Slaughter, ſiſter of Stephen Slaughter, painter: a preſent from miſs Anne Clement.

The virgin and child, and two angels holding tapers; an ancient carving in ivory: a preſent from Mr. Watſon the chirurgeon.

A lady's head, by Hilliard, unfiniſhed; bought at Mr. Lovibonde's.

A girl's head, in oil; very lively: by A. Cuyp.

George Hamilton, brother of count Antony Hamilton; ſmall copy in oil by E. Edwards, from the original in the poſſeſſion of lord Kingſland.

Print of Mr. W. Maſon, the poet.

A man's head in a black bonnet, æt. 30, 1539, by Holbein, unfiniſhed; bought at Mr. Lovibonde's.

A maſquerade at Vauxhall, in biſter; by lady Diana Beauclerc. There is wonderful expreſſion in the faces, and attitudes, though ſome of the figures are quite maſked, and others have half maſks.

A waſhed drawing of Les Rochers, the country-houſe of Mad. de Sevigné in Bretagne, done on the ſpot by Mr. Hinchliffe, ſon of the biſhop of Peterborough, in 1786.

Miſs Hannah More, the poeteſs; in water-colours, by Roberts, after Opie.

Miſs Farren, the comedian; in water-colours.

Two waſhed drawings, by miſs Agnes Berry.

View of Lee, the ſeat of T. Barrett, eſq. in Kent, by Pether; in an ebony frame.

A young Paris, caſt in terra-cotta, from a marble buſt by Mrs. Damer of the ſon of mademoiſelle Roſſi, a dancer.

Two old blue and white china jars; a candleſtick of Seve china; tea-things of old china; a ſmall tripod of or moulu to burn incenſe; and a red velvet purſe embroidered with gold and old French arms, to hold counters.

THE GREEN CLOSET.

IN the windows are ſome very curious pieces of painted glaſs. One round pane (one of the beſt in the houſe) repreſents the ſtory of the law-giver, who

who having enacted a law for punifhing adultery with blindnefs, and his own fon being convicted of it, he gave up one of his own eyes to fave one of his fon's. The drawing is fine, and the figures of the legiflator and of the young foldier who contemplates him, are evidently taken from fome picture or defign which gave the hint to Vandyck for his Belifarius, now at Chifwick. There are other curious panes: one with a rofe impaling a pomegranate, the device of Henry VIII. and Catharine of Arragon; others with a crown in a thorn-bufh between the letters H and E, the device of Henry VII. which he affumed after the battle of Bofworth, where Richard's crown was found in that manner. Over the door,

A view of Mr. Pope's houfe at Twickenham, painted fince the alterations made by fir William Stanhope; by Scott in his very beft manner. On the fame fide of the room are the following pictures, moft of them fmall:

A portrait of Sarah Malcolm, who was hanged for murdering her miftrefs and two other women in the Temple. She is fitting at a table in Newgate with popifh beads before her. This was drawn by Hogarth the day before her execution, and fhe had put on red to look the better.

Four landfcapes in water-colours, by Baudin.

A landfcape in needle-work, by lady Ailefbury, after Van Uden.

Eight views of ruins at Rome and other places, by Lucatelli.

A landfcape in Indian ink, with Italian, Chinefe and Gothic buildings; by Mr. Bentley, in his beft ftyle.

The head of old Dahl the painter, in water-colours, by himfelf; oval.

Cibber the ftatuary, with a pair of compaffes in his hand, in water-colours; by Chriftian Richter.

George Granville, lord Lanfdown, in red; ditto; by Vertue, after Kneller.

Two fmall pictures in oil, the ftories of Sufanna and the elders, and of David and Bathfheba: Italian.

A beggar-boy with a bird's-neft, water-colours on ivory; by Mr. Horace Walpole, from Murillo.

Queen Henrietta Maria; by Dixon.

Mary princefs of Orange, mother of king William; by Hofkins.

Sir Robert Walpole and Catherine lady Walpole; heads carved in ivory.

An

An old head, in a laced night-cap and ruff; by Cornelius Janſen, or Porbus.

Lady Arabella Stuart, when a child; by Iſaac Oliver.

Zachary Kneller, brother of ſir Godfrey; by Vertue, after Kneller.

St. Catherine reading; after Correggio, by Catherine lady Walpole.

At the end fronting the window:

A pot of carnations, drawn at Chelſea from the life by Van Huyſum, who lived there two years with ſir Robert Walpole: he was brother to the famous flower-painter: in oil.

Robert Walpole, father of ſir Robert Walpole; a head in crayons.

Mary Burwell, his wife; ditto.

An herb-market and a fiſh-market; after Teniers, in oil, by Angelis.

Sir Jeffery Burwell, grandfather of ſir Robert Walpole; he is an old man ſitting; a death's head by him: in crayons.

Mary, his wife, daughter and coheireſs of Thomas Derehaugh of Colton-hall, Suffolk: in crayons.

A ſtable-yard, with a cart, and a woman paring turnips; by J. H. Muntz; in oil.

Six curious pictures in water-colours of Mary de Medici and Louis XIII. and five great ducheſſes of Tuſcany; copied from a chamber at Poggio Imperiale near Florence, where the originals are dreſſed in the very clothes they wore, paſted on the hangings, with the faces painted on ſattin.

Six more drawings of ruins, by Lucatelli.

Anna Chamber counteſs Temple; by Hamilton.

Henry Carey earl of Monmouth, knight of the bath, tranſlator of many works *; by Theodore Ruſſel.

* See his article in the Catalogue of Royal and Noble Authors.

Pope

Pope Benedict XIII. in wax; behind it is his elogium, written by Mr. Walpole and printed in his Fugitive Pieces.

Lady Newburgh, lord Lansdown's Myra, in widow's weeds; copied by young Lens from the original of sir Godfrey Kneller, in the collection of the earl of Cardigan; in water-colours.

The countess of Buckingham, mother of duke George Villiers, in mourning; by ditto: from the same collection.

Anna Maria Brudenel countess of Shrewsbury, famous for her amours with the second George Villiers duke of Buckingham; by ditto, from ditto.

James Stuart duke of Richmond and earl of Litchfield, husband of the beautiful Mrs. Stuart whom Charles II. was in love with; in armour; by Cooper.

Susan Airmine lady Bellasis, mistress of James II.; by Cooper, unfinished.

Lady Anne Watson, daughter of Thomas earl of Strafford; by ditto.

Spencer Compton earl of Northampton, killed in the civil war.

A lady's head, temp. James I.

Two ladies of the court of queen Elizabeth; by Hilliard. These five belonged to Spencer Compton earl of Wilmington.

An infant's head, sleeping, by Vischer; very natural: in black lead.

A boy's head, in red and black chalks; by Peter Oliver: very lively.

Mrs. Catherine Clive, the excellent comedian, in the character of the Fine Lady in Lethe; in water-colours by Worlidge.

A lady's head; in a black hood; by Cooper.

Boncourt, a French comedian; given by the comte du Chatelet.

A gentleman's head, in oil; oval, in a metal case.

Thomas earl of Arundel; small head, in oil.

Charles II. in robes of the garter; in water-colours, after Lely; done by Richard second lord Edgecumbe at the age of sixteen.

Two

Two pieces of fruit and flowers, in water-colours; by old Lens.

Mrs. Scott, the painter's wife; by Deacon. A gentleman of great genius for drawing, who having misfortunes took to painting portraits in miniature, and hired the houſe late Zincke's in Covent-Garden, where Mr. Meyer the enameller now lives; but Mr. Deacon died in a year by the jail-diſtemper which was brought to the Old Bailey, where he happened to attend.

Mr. Pope, by young Lens, in water-colours; round.

Pomona; by Clinkſted.

Mr. Thomas Gray; etched from his ſhade; by Mr. W. Maſon.

A landſcape on copper; by Roland Savery.

Lord Herbert of Cherbury; a print coloured by Wale, from the original of Iſaac Oliver, in the collection of lord Powis.

William lord Mansfield; in oil, by Wootton.

Zeeman junior, painter, in blue, by his father.

Profile of an angel, after Guido; done in hair by Mary Lane, 1778.

Impreſſion of Oliver Cromwell's privy ſeal.

The two ſons of the old Pretender; painted at Rome in 1740.

The viſcount Stafford, beheaded in the reign of Charles II.; in water-colours; a preſent from Mr. E. Jerningham the poet, nearly related to the Staffords.

On the window-ſide fronting the door, beginning on the left-hand

A view of the Thames from Mrs. Clive's houſe at Twickenham; in blue and white, by Muntz.

A ſprig of orange-flowers, and another of apple-bloſſoms; by Catherine lady Walpole, in water-colours.

A bunch of white roſes; by ditto.

Inſide of a church, by Steenwick.

Four more views of ruins; by Lucatelli.

A Chineſe building, deſigned and drawn by Mr. Bentley for the corner of the wood at Strawberry-hill, where the chapel now ſtands; in Indian ink.

The Farneſe Hercules, in wax; by Goſſet.

Cleopatra, in water-colours; Italian.

Mrs. Beale, and her ſon Charles; heads in water-colours by her.

Profile head of a Magdalen, a coloured print by Le Blon.

A red and white roſe, executed in feathers, by Werman Cany.

Biſhop Burnet in robes of prelate of the garter; by Mrs. Roſe.

Prince Charles of Lorrain, in a frame of tortoiſe-ſhell.

Then paſs to the right hand.

Over the window, B. Hoadley biſhop of Wincheſter, in wax; by Goſſet: and

Charles Townſhend chancellor of the exchequer: ditto.

Boors reading: Flemiſh. It was in ſir Robert Walpole's collection.

A landſcape: by Teniers.

Two more views of ruins: by Lucatelli.

The arms of ſir Robert Walpole and Catherine Shorter, cut in paper on looking-glaſs, by Bermingham.

A converſation, after Watteau, in water-colours; by Mr. Horace Walpole.

Deſign for the arms of the two clubs at White's; drawn by the ſecond lord Edgecumbe, and invented by him, Mr. G. A. Selwyn, Mr. Geo. J. Williams, and Mr. Hor. Walpole, at Strawberry-hill. The arms are as follow: Vert (for the card-table) on a chevron ſable (for the hazard table) two rouleaus of guineas in ſaltire between two dice proper, the chevron between 3 parolis at Pharaoh, proper; on a canton ſable, a white balloting-ball. Creſt, an arm and hand holding a dice-box, iſſuant from an earl's coronet. Supporters, an old and a young knave of clubs (for the two clubs). Motto, *cog-it amor nummi.* The arms ſurrounded by a bottle-ticket inſcribed, *claret*, in the manner of an order.

A king-fiſher and ducks, of the Batterſea enamel: it was a manufacture ſtamped with a copper-plate, ſupported by alderman Janſen, but failed.

Charles II. young, in armour, with the garter; oval miniature.

Mary ducheſs of Beaufort: oval miniature.

Mr. Congreve, in armour: oil.

A lady, with Italian mottoes; in a round.

A friar and lady at her toilette; by Clinkſted.

A woman hiding her lover from her blind huſband; by ditto.

A woman fainting in a man's arms; after ſome great maſter: D. Rawdon fe. 1703.

Mr. Deacon's ſon, by him: unfiniſhed.

Drawing by Müntz, in water-colours, from an illumination to a book of earl Rivers in the library at Lambeth, and from which the frontiſpiece was taken to Mr. Walpole's Catalogue of Royal and Noble Authors.

At the end of the cloſet towards the Thames.

Over the window, impreſſion of the great ſeal of queen Henrietta Maria: and

Frederic prince of Wales, in wax; by Goſſet.

Two prints of old Stocks-market, and Eſſex-court in the Temple, coloured by Baudin.

Head of James firſt earl of Stanhope, in crayons.

Ditto of Mrs. Sclater, in a black gauze hood.

Four more views, by Lucatelli. There are 24 in all.

Sir John Shorter, grandfather of Catherine lady Walpole; in crayons.

He was lord-mayor in 1688, when receiving the pope's nuntio in the city, James II. gave him an additional quarter to his arms: two years before he had been one of the moſt diſtinguiſhed aldermen on the Whig ſide. He died in his mayoralty.

Iſabella Birkhead, his widow, in weeds. They are buried in the church of St. Saviour, Southwark. Vide Maitland's Hiſtory of London.

Mary Bruce ducheſs of Richmond; by Hamilton.

Anne Conway, daughter of general Conway and lady Aileſbury, and wife of John Damer, eldeſt ſon of Joſeph lord Milton; by Hamilton.

Octagon of Thomas earl of Southampton, in his robes; but quære whether it is not the laſt duke of Ormond but one?

Henry Howard earl of Northampton; copied in water-colours by Hardinge; from the original at the earl's college at Greenwich.

A ſmall half-length of a young man, octagon on copper, by Fr. Hals; from Mr. Jennings's collection.

Two landſcapes in ſoot-water; by Mr. Bentley.

A writing-box, richly carved in ivory.

Two blue and white jars.

A red velvet coffer ornamented with ſilver, and containing ſix dram-bottles of the old Venetian glaſs flowered with gold and enamelled tops; from Mrs. Kennon's collection.

A temple of old japan.

Two cups and ſaucers of Seve china.

A ſmall table of ditto.

Three ebony chairs.

Small bronze buſt of Caracalla*.

Profile of lady Aileſbury, in wax; by her daughter Mrs. Damer.

* In the cupboards in this cloſet are many MSS. particularly all thoſe of Vertue, which Mr. Walpole bought of his widow.

Thomas

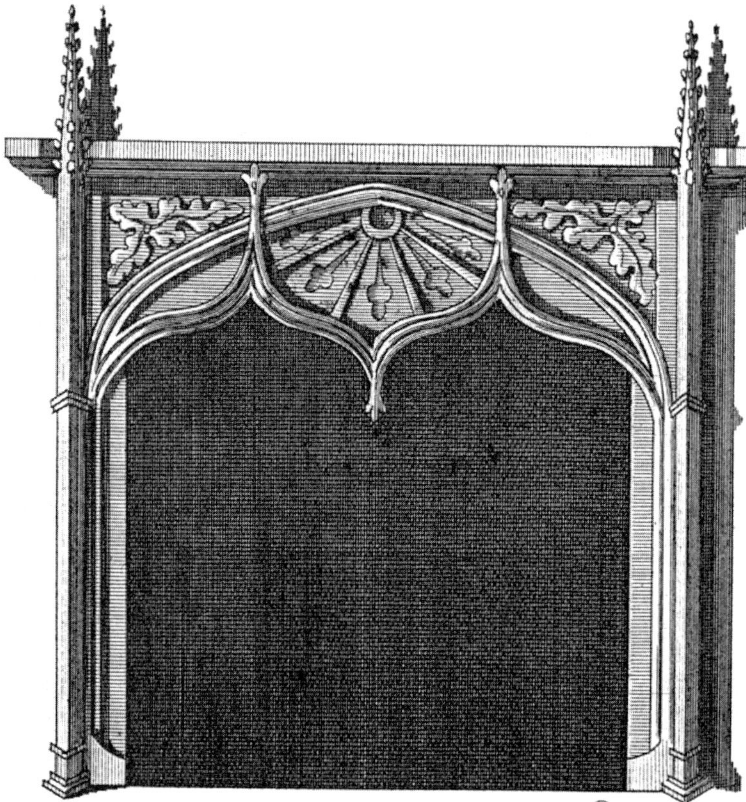

J. Morris sc.

CHIMNEY IN THE BLUE BED CHAMBER.

Thomas Seymour lord Sudley, brother of the protector Somerſet, copied by lady Lucan from the original in the poſſeſſion of the marquis of Buckingham.

Mary Churchill, ſecond wife of Charles lord Cadogan; ſmall life in oil, by W. Stavely.

A waſhed drawing of the walnut-tree covered with ivy on the terrace at Strawberry-hill, in winter; by lady Diana Beauclerc.

Two kittens in marble, by Mrs. Damer.

THE BLUE BED-CHAMBER.

HUNG with plain blue paper; a linen bed; eight chintz chairs; a toilette worked by Mrs. Clive; a looking-glaſs in a tortoiſeſhell frame, ornamented with ſilver; two blue and white ſquare candleſticks of old Delft ware: an ancient lock to the door, richly wrought of braſs and ſteel; and a cabinet japanned by lady Walpole: on it, an ewer and baſon of blue and white Seve china; under it a blue and gold china bottle.

The chimney-piece was deſigned by Mr. Bentley. Over it,

In a frame of black and gold carved by Gibbons, ſir Robert Walpole and Catherine Shorter; ſmall whole lengths; by Eckardt, after Zincke: the hounds and view of Houghton by Wootton. Sir Robert is ſitting; by him, on a table, is the purſe of chancellor of the exchequer, leaning againſt buſts of George I. and II. to denote his being firſt miniſter to thoſe kings: by lady Walpole are flowers, ſhells, a pallet and pencils, to mark her love of the arts. On the chimney,

A boy and girl in Seve biſcuit.

Three ſmall flower-pots, ditto.

Two cups and ſaucers, ditto.

Four blue and white cream-cups.

In the bow window, ſome very beautiful painted glaſs.

General Henry Seymour Conway, and Caroline countess dowager of Ailesbury, his wife; their daughter Anne sitting on the ground playing with a dog. The attitudes and dresses taken from Watteau. This, and all the other pictures in this room, were painted by Eckardt.

Charles Churchill, and lady Maria Walpole, his wife, with their eldest son Charles; taken from the picture at Blenheim, of Rubens, his wife and child.

Sir Charles Hanbury Williams, knight of the bath.

Mr. Thomas Gray *; taken from the portrait of a musician by Vandyck, at the duke of Grafton's.

Mr. Richard Bentley; from Vandyck. He holds in one hand his own design of the figure of Melancholy drawn by him for the edition of Mr. Gray's Odes.

Mr. Horace Walpole; from Vandyck, leaning on the Ædes Walpolianæ: behind him, a view of Strawberry-hill. The frames are of black and gold, carved after those to Lombard's prints from Vandyck, but with emblems peculiar to each person.

THE RED BEDCHAMBER.

HUNG with crimson paper; by the bed, a crucifix of ivory; an ewer and bason of Chantilli porcelaine; a red and white flower-pot, cup, saucer and sugar-dish, of Seve porcelaine; crimson Norwich damask chairs, and an arm-chair of patch-work.

Pictures on the chimney side:

Gypsies telling a country-maiden her fortune at the entrance of a beech-wood; a most beautiful drawing in water-colours, designed and executed by lady Diana Beauclerc in 1781; the chef-d'œuvre of her works.

A drawing in Indian-ink of a forest, by Mary Danby, first married to Mr. Lockhart, and afterwards to general Harcourt, only brother of George Simon second earl of Harcourt.

* With this motto, alluding to an Ode on Eton, which, though one of his best productions, was his first published, *Nec licuit populis parvum te, Nile, videre.*

An

An old beggar; by Teniers.

Heads of goats, a fine ſketch by Berghem; from the collection of Wootton the painter.

View of Elizabeth-caſtle in Jerſey, by Müntz; in oil.

A coloured drawing, by the reverend Mr. Gilpin.

Maria Walpole counteſs of Waldegrave and ducheſs of Glouceſter, with her eldeſt danghter lady Elizabeth Laura; a mezzotinto.

A moonlight on copper, by Bonus, jun.

Side oppoſite the window.

A landſcape, by Mullins.

Falconet the painter's wife, by him; highly finiſhed.

Mary Kirk, wife of ſir Richard Vernon, known by the name of Warmeſtre in the Memoires de Grammont.

Two views of Richmond-hill, and Twickenham, from Strawberry-hill, by Müntz; in oil.

Le comte de Grignan; a print.

Madame de Caylus, niece of madame de Maintenon; a print.

Two old men; an Italian ſketch.

The original drawing of Titus Oates, in black lead, by Robert White; a preſent from Richard Bull, eſq.

A head of the duke d'Epernon, favourite of Henry III. painted on oriental alabaſter; a preſent from colonel St. Paul, chargé d'affaires at Paris.

A print of the princeſs Sophia, eldeſt daughter of their royal highneſſes William Henry and Maria, duke and ducheſs of Glouceſter.

The father of Pope as he lay dead; drawn by his father-in-law Samuel Cooper: bought by Richardſon, junior, at the ſale of Mrs. Martha Blount, to whom Pope had bequeathed this and the three following.

Mrs.

Mrs. Editha Cooper, mother of Pope; by John Richardſon, ſenior.

Mr. Pope himſelf; ditto.

Henry St. John viſcount Bolingbroke; ditto.

Sketch by Kent, for a niche in Mr. Fairfax's houſe in Saville-row.

On the ſides of the window:

Madame de Prie, miſtreſs of the duc de Bourbon, prime miniſter in the minority of Louis XV. in crayons; ſhe died of vexation at the diſgrace of the duke: a preſent from madame du Deffand, who was intimate with her.

The four ſeaſons, heads of boys in rounds; Italian: a preſent from the duc de Nivernois.

Macbeth in the witches' cave; a print.

Four drawings of humour, waſhed, by Elias Martin.

An ancient illuminated drawing.

A landſcape, view in Jerſey, by Mr. Bentley; in oil *.

A young lady reading the Caſtle of Otranto to her companion; a graceful and expreſſive drawing, done for a preſent to Mr. W. by Lavinia Bingham, eldeſt daughter of lady Lucan the celebrated copyiſt, and ſince married to lord Althorp.

A fine drawing in water-colours, by the reverend Mr. Gilpin.

Sophia Dorothea, wife of George the firſt; copied by Hardinge from the original which princeſs Amelie bequeathed to her nephew the landgrave of Heſſe, and which George the ſecond hung up in Leiceſter-houſe as ſoon as he heard of his father's death.

A ſmall head of Oldham, the poet, in oil; as clear and fine as Vandyck. It had been in the collection of Mr. Dinely.

A view of lady Di. Beauclerc's villa at Twickenham, by Sam. Lyſons, eſq.

* In this piece Mr. Bentley has repreſented himſelf and his ſecond wife on the ſea ſhore.

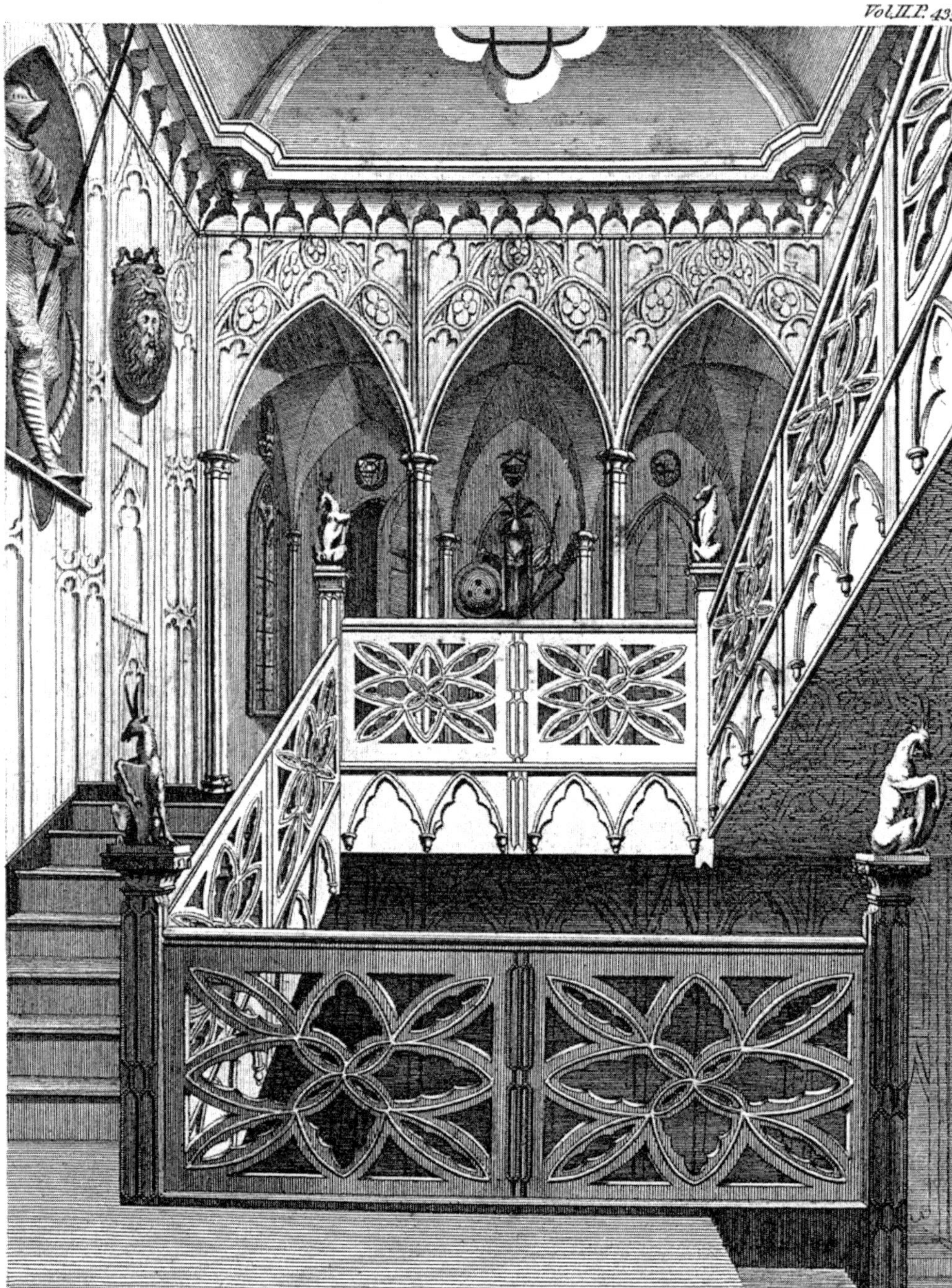

E. Edwards delin.

J. Newton sculpsit

STAIRCASE AT STRAWBERRY HILL.

ON THE STAIRCASE.

IN a niche, the armour of Francis I. king of France, of ſteel gilt, and covered with bas-reliefs in a fine taſte: his lance is of ebony inlaid with ſilver; his ſword ſteel; beautifully inlaid with gold, probably the work of Benvenuto Cellini: there is alſo the armour for the horſe's head. This very valuable ſuit of armour was purchaſed from the Crozat collection in 1772, on the death of the baron de Thiers, when the czarina bought the fine collection of pictures and bronzes. Over againſt it,

Henry V. and his family; bought in 1773, at the ſale of James Weſt, preſident of the Royal Society. See a deſcription and print of this picture in the firſt volume of the Anecdotes of Painting in England. This picture came out of Stafford-houſe, or Tart-hall, Weſtminſter: and I imagine that this, and the two others of Henry VI. and VII. were done by order of Henry VII. in honour of the houſe of Lancaſter. I have heard that that of Henry VI. came out of the palace of Shene.

Henry VIII. aged 29, and Charles V. aged 20, in one picture, from Mr. Weſt's collection. Behind Charles V. are two figures, probably deſigned for his grandfather and father, the emperor Maximilian, and Philip.

Two ſhields of leather, for tournaments, painted by Polidore; one has the head of Meduſa, the other of Perſeus: on the inſides are battles in gold. They came out of the collection of commendatore Vittoria at Naples, and were ſent to Mr. W. by ſir W. Hamilton, with a third of iron, repreſenting the ſtory of Curtius, but certainly not antique, as there is a cannon and an embattled tower at a diſtance.

Over the middle arcade is a curious ancient head of Henry III. carved in alto-relievo on oak, from the church of Barnwell near Oundle in Northamptonſhire, which he endowed. This head is very like to the effigies on his tomb, and to that in painted glaſs in the chapel here at Strawberry-hill.

Monamy the painter ſhewing a ſea-piece to Mr. Thomas Walker, a collector of pictures; ſmall life; the figures by Hogarth, the ſea-piece by Monamy. A preſent from Richard Bull, eſq.

A Perſian ſhield, over the door into the blue room.

An ancient diſh of fayence, over the door of the red room.

Top of a warming-pan that belonged to Charles II. with his arms and this motto, *Sarve God and live for ever.* As the date on it is 1660, with C. R. it probably was uſed for his majeſty and the ducheſs of Cleveland.

Wootton the painter, his wife and children; ſmall life, painted by Gav. Hamilton.

THE ARMOURY

IS an open veſtibule of three gothic arches, lighted by a window entirely of painted glaſs, and ornamented over the doors and niches with quarterings of the family of Walpole, painted by Grant.

Two ſuits of armour, on one of which is the mark of a bullet; two helmets; a gauntlet; a round leathern quiver; and two pair of ſtirrups; from Coombe, near Kingſton in Surry, which ſeat formerly belonged to the great Richard Neville earl of Warwick. Theſe arms therefore probably were part of thoſe which ſerved his troops when he marched to Weſtminſter to awe the parliament in the reign of Henry the Sixth.

A beautiful Perſian ſhield, made of a rhinoceros's hide tanned, enamelled, and almoſt tranſparent.

An Indian ſcimitar, the handles and ornaments of ſilver, in a green velvet caſe; and a dagger of the ſame; given by a nabob to George Morton Pitt, governor of Fort St. George, and by his widow to Mr. Walpole.

An Indian ſword, the blade waving and damaſked, the ſcabbard of wood twiſted with cane, the hilt an owl carved in wood.

Two Indian quivers, full of arrows.

An Indian lance, the head of wood double-barbed and delicately wrought, that it might break into ſplinters in a wound.

Several other lances, ſpears, and Indian bows.

An

An Indian bow, painted.

An Indian ſcimitar in a Japan ſcabbard.

Four broad ſwords.

A collar ſet with ſpikes, for a wild beaſt.

Five pieces of a coat of mail.

An Indian pouch made of beads and hair; a girdle, ditto; a collar, ditto; and two leather ſhoes, ornamented ditto.

An eaſtern powder-horn of ſteel and bronze, richly graved, and hung to a chain with a tablet of bronze, characters in the middle on a red ground.

An Indian mace, inlaid with braſs.

A hatchet, ditto. Theſe three from the collection of monſ. Julienne at Paris.

Two halberds, from the old houſe at Houghton.

An American calumet; a warrior's wreath; and a neck ornament: preſents from governor Pownall.

An ancient muſket, richly carved; a preſent from Moſes Franks, eſq.

Another ancient muſket and piſtol inlaid with ivory; from the collection of Mr. Scott.

A tall oſſuarium with bas-reliefs, a ſacrifice and tripods.

Another, curious for being a double one; the inſcriptions,

VIBIA. P. L.	P. VIBIVS.
ASIATICE.	P. Ɔ. L.
VIXIT.	MODESTVS.
ANN. XXII.	

Head of Iſis, ſmall model in terra-cotta by Mrs. Damer, which ſhe executed in large in ſtone for the bridge at Henley.

An ancient battle-axe and a bandelier.

A curious royal lock, made as early as in the reign of Henry VII. from one of the palaces; a present from Thomas Aſtle, eſq.

The LIBRARY.

THE books are ranged within Gothic arches of pierced work, taken from a ſide-door caſe to the choir in Dugdale's St. Paul's. The doors themſelves were deſigned by Mr. Chute. The chimney-piece is imitated from the tomb of John of Eltham earl of Cornwall, in Weſtminſter-abbey: the ſtone-work from that of Thomas duke of Clarence, at Canterbury. An ancient curfeu, or couvre-feu; from Mr. Goſtling's collection. The ceiling was painted by Clermont, from Mr. Walpole's deſign drawn out by Mr. Bentley. In the middle is the ſhield of Walpole ſurrounded with the quarters borne by the family. At each end in a round is a knight on horſeback, in the manner of ancient ſeals; that next to the window bears the arms of Fitz Oſbert, the other of Robſart. At the four corners are ſhields, helmets, and mantles: on one ſhield is a large H, on another a W, ſemée of croſs croſslets, in imitation of an ancient bearing of the Howards in Blomfield's Norfolk. On another ſhield is the Saracen's head, the creſt of the family, but here the Catherine-wheel is above the cap, not on it; having been ſo borne by the Robſarts, as appears from the tomb of Lodowic Robſart lord Bourchier, in Weſtminſter-abbey. On the fourth ſhield is an antelope, one of lord Orford's ſupporters, with the arms about his neck, reſting under a tree, as in old devices. On either ſide is the motto of the family, *Fari quæ ſentiat*; and at the ends, M.DCC.LIV. the year in which this room was finiſhed, expreſſed in Gothic letters: the whole on a moſaic ground.

The large window and the two roſe windows have a great deal of fine painted glaſs, particularly, Faith, Hope, and Charity, whole figures in colours; a large ſhield with the arms of England, and heads of Charles I. and Charles II.

On one ſide of the window, a landſcape by Polemberg. Oppoſite to it,

Chriſtina queen of Sweden, in her uſual dreſs, partly male, partly female; a curious drawing with a pen by Steph. de la Bella.

Over the chimney, an ancient and valuable piece, repreſenting the mar-

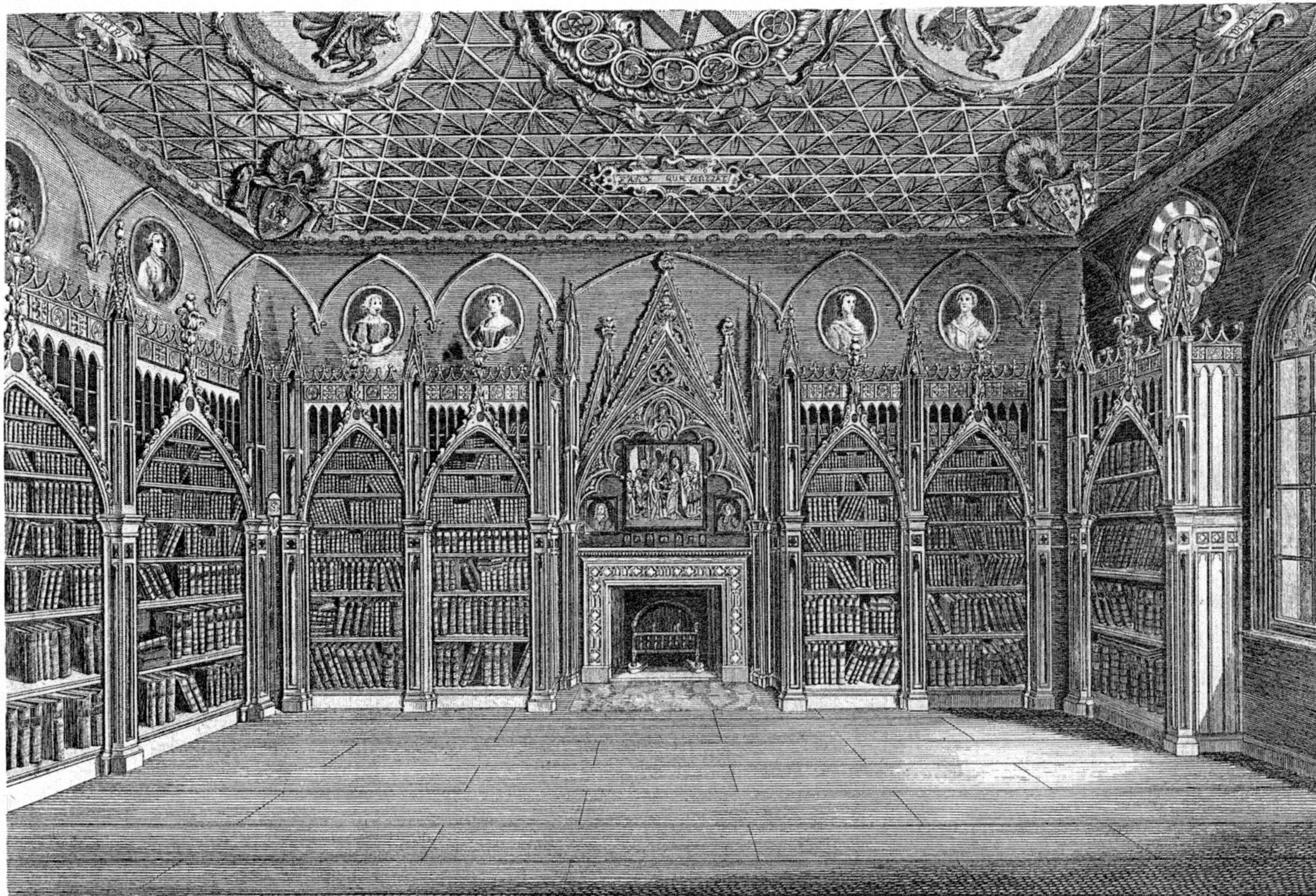

Godfrey Sculp.

Library
at Strawberry Hill.

riage of Henry VI. of which ſee a deſcription in The Anecdotes of Painting. Above it are that king's arms, the red roſe crowned, and queen Margaret's arms in a lozenge. On each ſide, two bronze medallions of the Malateſtas, ſovereigns of Rimini.

A girl and cat, in water-colours, copied by Mr. Walpole from Roſalba.

A boy with a flute, by ditto, from a picture of Cavalier Luti, at Houghton.

Sir Robert Walpole, when a boy, in crayons.

Sir Edward Walpole, knight of the bath, grandfather of ſir Robert; in oil.

Henry duke of Richmond, natural ſon of Henry VIII. in his ſhirt and night-cap, which is embroidered with black: a miniature.

Mary, ſole daughter and heireſs of Thomas lord Fairfax, wife of George Villiers ſecond duke of Buckingham: ditto, by Cooper.

The queen of Bohemia, daughter of James I. ditto, by Iſaac Oliver.

Sir Francis Drake: ditto, by Hilliard.

Charles Howard, earl of Nottingham, the great admiral, æt. 37; by Iſaac Oliver.

Lady Penelope Compton, daughter of Spencer earl of Northampton, and wife of ſir Edward Nicholas, ſecretary of ſtate; by Cooper.

Count Gondomar, a fine head in oil; ſmall.

A print of king Staniſlaus in his old age, coloured and dreſſed with ſilks after the clothes he wore: a preſent from Mrs. Damer.

A Roman ſimpulum in bronze.

Two bronze antique lamps and chains.

One ditto, modern, with a triton.

A cow, ditto.

An ancient braſs padlock in the ſhape of a hand.

A greyhound in bronze, to keep down papers.

 A ſilver

A ſilver ſtandiſh that was ſir Robert Walpole's, with his arms.

Pictures over the book-caſes:

Lady Fairborne, daughter of ſir —— Rookeſby, and wife of ſir Stafford Fairborne; in red: niece of

Catherine, daughter of Edward Darcy, eſq. and wife of ſir Eraſmus Philips, of Picton-caſtle in Pembrokeſhire, grandmother of Catherine lady Walpole, whom ſhe educated.

Sir John Shorter, lord mayor of London in 1688; in black.

Iſabella Birkhead, his wife.

Francis Seymour Conway earl of Hertford, and knight of the garter; by Aſtley, after Liotard.

Lady Iſabella Fitzroy, youngeſt daughter of Charles ſecond duke of Grafton, and wife of Francis earl of Hertford; by Eckardt, after Vanloo.

Henry Seymour Conway, only brother of lord Hertford: in armour, by Eckardt.

Charlotte, ſecond daughter of John Shorter of Bybrook in Kent, and third wife of Francis lord Conway; in yellow.

Thomas Shorter, ſecond ſon of ſir John Shorter; in brown.

John Shorter, eſq. of Bybrook in Kent, eldeſt ſon of ſir John Shorter; in red.

John Shorter, in armour, eldeſt ſon of the foregoing, and brother of

Catherine Shorter, eldeſt daughter of John Shorter of Bybrook, and firſt wife of ſir Robert Walpole afterwards earl of Orford: a copy after old Dahl.

A clock of ſilver gilt, richly chaſed, engraved and ornamented with fleurs de lys, little heads, &c. on the top ſits a lion holding the arms of England, which are alſo on the ſides. This was a preſent from Henry VIII. to Anne Boleyn; and ſince, from lady Elizabeth Germaine to Mr. Walpole. On the

the weights are the initial letters of Henry and Anne, within true lovers knots; at top, *Dieu et mon Droit.*

A ſemicircular oſſuarium, an uncommon form: in the pediment, a tripod ſupported by grifons: at each corner, a horned head of a man and a bird, a feſtoon hangs from the horns of the men, on which are two more birds: the inſcription,

P. LENILIO
MARTIALI
POSVIT FORTVNATVS
PATRONO SVO B. M.

A ſquare oſſuarium; heads of rams, a feſtoon and birds; the inſcription,

D. Q. I. C. L. M.
FECIT MCEEI
CAEIIAPRI
MIGENIAPD.

Theſe two urns were in the collection of doctor Meade.

An oſſuarium adorned on the front and ſides with ivy and birds drinking out of a vaſe; the inſcription,

D. TI. CL. M. SVCCESSO. FILIO. PIENTISSIMO. QVI.
ANN. VIX. XIIX. PARENTES FEC.

Three more, ſquare; and one round, with a bird on the cover.

The fiſhing eagle, modelled in terra-cotta, the ſize of life. This bird was taken in lord Melbourn's park at Brocket-hall, and in taking it one of the wings was almoſt cut off, and Mrs. Damer ſaw it in that momentary rage, which ſhe remembered, and has executed exactly. She has written her own name in Greek on the baſe, and Mr. W. added this line,

Non me Praxiteles finxit, at Anna Damer, 1787.

Rare books of prints and drawings in the library:

Thuanus, the large edition in 14 volumes, enriched with beautiful prints of of the beſt impreſſions, containing portraits of the principal perſonages. This ſet was collected by ſir Clement Cotterel Dormer.

Ædes Walpolianæ, the original drawings, with every print that has been engraved from the pictures, and with other prints and drawings of houſes and buildings that belonged to ſir Robert Walpole and the family of Walpole.

A collection of initial letters from the beginning of printing, with ſome drawings of heads of the firſt printers; collected by Mr. Ames, author of the Typographical Antiquities.

Sir Julius Cæſar's travelling library, containing 44 ſmall volumes in Latin, incloſed in a caſe the ſize of a folio.

Faithorne's works, moſt beautiful impreſſions; folio.

Hogarth's ditto; the moſt complete ſet of his works that is known, with ſome of his original drawings.

Mr. Henry Bunbury's ditto, in two volumes.

Vertue's ditto, in two large folios.

Teniers's ditto.

Twenty-one large volumes of prints after different great maſters.

A volume of drawings by Mr. Sam. Scott and Mr. Müntz.

Three volumes of Hollar's prints.

Drawings of the Florentine gallery.

Prints from pictures, antiquities and curioſities, at Strawberry-hill.

Drawings by Italian maſters, bound in red morocco, 3 vols.

Drawings and prints of heads of Engliſh painters and artiſts, in 2 volumes folio: very curious.

Twelve large folios of Engliſh heads, bound in vellum, and ranged according to the reign of each king.

Five

Five larger of the reign of George III. and an additional volume of heads of different reigns collected ſince.

A volume of heads, antiquities, monuments, views, &c. by Vertue and others.

Deſigns by Mr. Richard Bentley, bound in marble and gilt.

Ditto by Rembrandt, Van Huyſum, &c.

Proceſſion of knights of the garter, temp. queen Elizabeth, copied by Vertue from the originals by Mark Garrard.

Sevigniana, or a collection of portraits of ſeveral perſons mentioned in the letters of madame de Sevigné.

A book of French portraits in the time of Francis I. It belonged to Brantome, who has inſcribed the names of ſeveral of the perſons. From the collection of monſieur Mariette at Paris.

A large volume bound in red morocco and gold, containing etchings by various perſons of quality.

A large book of miſcellaneous drawings by various maſters, ancient and modern.

Curious books in the glaſs cloſet in the library:

Mr. Bentley's original deſigns for Mr. Gray's poems, bound in red morocco and gilt.

Six views after nature in Indian-ink, by Bernard Lens.

A book of patterns for old point lace; exceedingly rare.

Baker on Learning, with MS. notes.

Holbein's prints for the bible, with French verſes by Nicholas Borbonius.

Drawings of all the Spintrian medals; from ſir Clem. Cotterel's library.

Apologie de Jehan Chaſtel: very rare.

Milton's

Milton's Paradiſe Loſt, given by the duke of Wharton to lady Mary Wortley Montagu, who has written verſes in the firſt leaf.

A miſſal, engraved on copper-plates at Venice.

D'Eon's Letters, with prints of the principal perſons: quarto.

Callot's pocket-book, with a great number of exquiſite original drawings by himſelf: a preſent to Mr. Walpole from his brother Robert earl of Orford: very valuable.

Bizarie di varie figure di Giovan Batiſta Bracelli, pittore Fiorentino al Illmo. S. Don Pietro Medici: 1624. This moſt rare and ſingular book contains prints of human figures formed by the ſtrangeſt materials, as diamonds, hoops, bladders, pieces of carpentry, battledoors, kitchen-ſtuff, &c. &c. It ſeems to be the compoſition of a madman, but the drawings are maſterly, and the attitudes moſt noble.

Le tombeau de Marguerite de Valois, with verſes by three daughters of the protector duke of Somerſet: very ſcarce.

The pocket-book, with his expences, of Robert Walpole, father of ſir Robert Walpole.

Accounts of Blenheim, Stowe, Wilton, and other places, with MS. notes by Mr. Horace Walpole: tied in one parcel.

A German book with prints coloured of Charles V. and the German princes of his time.

The arms of the knights of the garter made by Richard III. in their proper colours, and bound in red velvet: a preſent from Walter Robertſon, mayor of Lynn.

Deſcription of Wilton, with drawings and notes by Vertue.

A book of heads and ſketches, by Vertue.

A complete ſet of the books printed at Strawberry-hill.

A book of drawings of vaſes, bas-reliefs, and other antiquities.

Catalogue of the Harleian collection with the prices, and drawings of ſome of the curioſities by Vertue.

Dr. Percy's book of the earl of Northumberland's houſehold.

Two books of ſwan-marks, on vellum: extremely rare.

A book of deſigns of buildings, by John Chute, eſq. of the Vine.

Drawings of churches, monuments, &c. by ſir Charles Frederick and Smart Lethullier, eſq. in 3 vols. folio.

A thin folio, containing 35 prints after groteſque paintings.

The Iliad and Odyſſey, the very books from which Pope made his tranſlations: in one of the volumes is a view of Twickenham, drawn by Pope.

Three illuminated miſſals.

Whiſton's Life, with MS. index of the principal paſſages.

Sir T. More's Life, with marginal writing by Philip earl of Pembroke.

The Charter of Foreſts, one of the original copies finely preſerved, with the great ſeal of Edward I. appendant; found at Hackney 1743, among writings of the ancient family of Shordich, by Robert Bygrave; preſented by him to ſir Edward Walpole, and by him to his brother Horace.

Bathoe's catalogues of the collections of Charles I. James II. and the duke of Buckingham; with their portraits, and large additions and notes by Mr. Walpole.

Catalogue of the pictures belonging to the crown, temp. Annæ, MS. A preſent from Mr. Topham Beauclerc.

Two large volumes of catalogues of all the exhibitions from the firſt, to the end of the year 1780, with MS. notes.

Catalogue of the 25 moſt precious coins and medals in the roſe-wood caſe.

1. An unique crown of king Edward VI. bought at lord Oxford's ſale in 1742.

2. Medal of pope Julius III. in ſilver, ſtruck on the reſtoration of the Roman catholic religion in England by queen Mary.

3. A ſatirical ſilver medal ſtruck in Holland. On the obverſe, the head of Oliver Cromwell laureated in armour. On the reverſe he is kneeling in the lap of Britannia, with his breeches down; the French and Spaniſh ambaſſadors are contending which ſhall kiſs firſt; the former ſays to the latter, *Retire toy, l'honneur appartient au roi mon maitre Louis le Grand.* Very ſcarce; from lord Oxford's collection.

4. A ſilver medal; on one ſide the head of queen Mary of England, on the other, of Philip II. both in alto-relievo, and of the moſt exquiſite workmanſhip. It was a trial-piece, and is certainly the fineſt modern medal known. It was bought by Mr. Walpole in Italy.

5. A large gold medal of Henry VIII. On the reverſe, his titles in Hebrew, Greek and Latin. It is the firſt medal of the Engliſh ſeries. From lord Oxford's collection.

6. A ſilver medal on the deſtruction of the Spaniſh armada. See an account of this medal, and the preceding, in Evelyn. From the ſame collection.

7. Coin of young king Henry, ſon of Henry II. From ditto.

8. Fine gilt coin of pope Paul III. Reverſe, a Ganymede, admirably drawn: this beautiful coin was the work of Michael Angelo Buonaroti. From the collection of baron Stoſch.

9. Silver medal of lord treaſurer Southampton; by Abraham Simon.

10. Gold fragment of queen Elizabeth's laſt broad piece, deſcribed in the Royal and Noble Authors. Unique: from the Oxford collection.

11. Gold medal of Nero Claudius Druſus: reverſe, trophies, *De Germanis.*

12. Gold medal of Trajan: reverſe, his forum. Theſe two are very rare.

13. Gold medal of Marc Antony: reverſe, the head of Octavia, the only one of her known, which makes this medal of the higheſt value.

14. Gold medal of Otho: very ſcarce, and finely preſerved.

15. Ditto of Pertinax: not only very rare, but in the moſt exquiſite preſervation.

16. Copper coin of king Ferdinand of Naples; a pun on the reverſe; his arms, a *horſe*; the motto, *Equitas regni.*

17. Silver coin of Euſtace, ſon of king Stephen; very rare: from lord Oxford's collection.

18. A ſilver half crown of pope Clement XI. Reverſe, the pantheon.

19. Copper medal of pope Gregory XIII. on the correction of the calendar: the reverſe, which is in beautiful taſte, was deſigned by Parmegiano.

20. Silver medal of the ſame pope, on the maſſacre of St. Barthelemi: on the reverſe, the deſtroying angel murdering the proteſtants; the legend, *Hugonotorum Strages*. This ſcandalous medal was called in, and the die broken; which has made it very uncommon.

21. A ſilver coin ſtruck by the republic of Florence when they declared Jeſus Chriſt their king, to keep off the pope: from baron Stoſch's collection: extremely rare.

22. Copper medal of Lorenzo of Medici, who ſtabbed duke Alexander: the reverſe copied from Brutus's medal, with the cap of liberty between two daggers; the legend, VIII *Id. Jan.* Very rare.

23. Copper medal of Clement VII. Reverſe, Joſeph and his brethren: deſigned by Raphael.

24. Coin of Theodore king of Corſica: rare.

25. Braſs ſatirical medal on queen Anne: reverſe, the queen and lady Maſham embracing; motto, *All for Love.*

Mr. WALPOLE's BEDCHAMBER, Two Pair of Stairs.

THE chimney-piece was deſigned by Mr. Chute, and has great grace. In the window, compoſed of ſeven lights, are ſeveral curious pieces of painted glaſs; as, the arms of Anne Boleyn with the quarterings which the king allowed her to bear of the families from which ſhe was deſcended, though with no right of quartering; a large lion coloured; four large angels in black and white; cypher and portcullis of king Edward; arms of Clinton and Ratcliffe; fine heads in black and white of Charlemagne, prince William, and prince Maurice of Orange, &c.

Over the chimney, View of the Vine in Hampſhire, the ſeat of John Chute, eſq. by Müntz.

A ſmall print of Mr. Andrews's Gothic houſe near Donnington-caſtle and Spine-hill, Berkſhire; deſigned by John Chute, eſq.

Fifteen ſmall drawings of Engliſh and French comedians; by Feſch.

View of the gate of St. Edmund at Bury.

A fable, in cut paper on looking-glaſs; by Bermingham.

Over the door, Head of John Chute, eſq. by Müntz, after Pompeio Battoni.

La ſignora Eliſabetta Capponi Griſoni, a Florentine beauty; by Ferd. Richter, 1741.

Patapan, a Roman dog, belonging to Mr. Walpole; by Wootton.

Doctor Conyers Middleton; by Eckardt.

Doctor Thomas Aſhton, fellow of Eton-college; by ditto. He died in 1775.

A man and woman in water-colours, after Watteau; by Mr. Walpole.

A rural ball, after Watteau; by ditto.

Catherine Walpole, eldeſt daughter of ſir Robert Walpole; ſmall head in oil.

Horace Walpole, when a child, in a white frock; in crayons.

A ſprig of orange, in water-colours; by lady Walpole.

A bunch of flowers, ditto; by lady Anne Conway, eldeſt daughter of lord Hertford, and wife of the earl of Drogheda.

Drawing of Rembrandt's mother, from the picture at Windſor, called the counteſs of Deſmond; by Müntz.

Prints, of the houſe of commons and warrant for beheading Charles I. inſcribed with a pen, *Major charta*; of Ethelreda lady Townſhend; of lord Chatham; lord Holland; lord and lady Strafford; Mr. H. Walpole; and le comte de Guerchy.

A cat, in an ebony frame.

A landſcape by Mr. Taverner, exactly in the manner of Gaſpar Pouſſin.

In the Plaid Bedchamber, in the South Tower, is the portrait of Henry Walpole the jeſuit, who was executed for attempting to poiſon queen Elizabeth. He is crowned with glory and holds a palm-branch, the emblem of martyrdom; the arms of the family in one corner. This picture came from Mr. Walpole's of Lincolnſhire, the laſt of the Roman catholic branch of the family, who died about the year 1748.

The STAR CHAMBER

IS a ſmall anti-room, painted green, with golden ſtars in moſaic. It has a large window entirely of painted glaſs; two triangular chairs taken from a piece of glaſs in Mr. Walpole's bed-chamber; two ſmall Welch armed chairs, painted blue and white, with cuſhions of point-lace, and on one the arms of Mr. Richard Bateman, at whoſe ſale they were purchaſed: a japan tea-table with white porcelaine; and a card-table of the ſame.

A mahogany cabinet, containing a collection of Engliſh and foreign coins and

and medals. On it, a buſt of Henry VII. in ſtone, a model in great taſte for his tomb, by Torreggiano*. Under it a vaſe of falſe porphyry; from the collection of the comte de Caylus.

Another like cabinet, with gold, ſilver, and braſs Greek and Roman coins, and a complete ſet of Roman weights from Dr. Middleton's collection. On it, a buſt of Gibbs the architect in marble, by Ryſbrack. Beneath, a vaſe, companion to the former.

A porringer, cover and plate, white, with different golds, of Seve china; a preſent from Mrs. Damer.

Catherine Haſtings, firſt counteſs of Cheſterfield.

Hence you go into a trunk-ceiled paſſage, lighted by a window of painted glaſs, in which are many quarterings of Latton, a family formerly ſeated at Eſher in Surry: in the window, a candleſtick enamelled on copper. This paſſage leads to

THE HOLBEIN CHAMBER.

THE ceiling is taken from the queen's dreſſing-room at Windſor. The chimney-piece, deſigned by Mr. Bentley, is chiefly taken from the tomb of archbiſhop Warham at Canterbury. Over it, a glaſs in a black and gold frame; and a piece of Roman fayence in the ſhape of a boat, Bacchus and Ceres in relief in the middle.

A fire-ſcreen embroidered by Miſs Hotham, to whom Mr. W. addreſſed the fable of The Magpie and her young.

Two blue china beakers.

The pierced arches of the ſcreen from the gates of the choir of Rouen; the reſt of the ſcreen was deſigned by Mr. Bentley.

In the bow windows ſome fine painted glaſs, and the arms of England, and thoſe of George prince of Denmark; the ground is a beautiful moſaic of crimſon, blue, and pearls, deſigned and painted by Price of Hatton-garden.

A table and ſix chairs of ebony. On the table a tray with four ancient

* Vide Anecdotes of Painting.

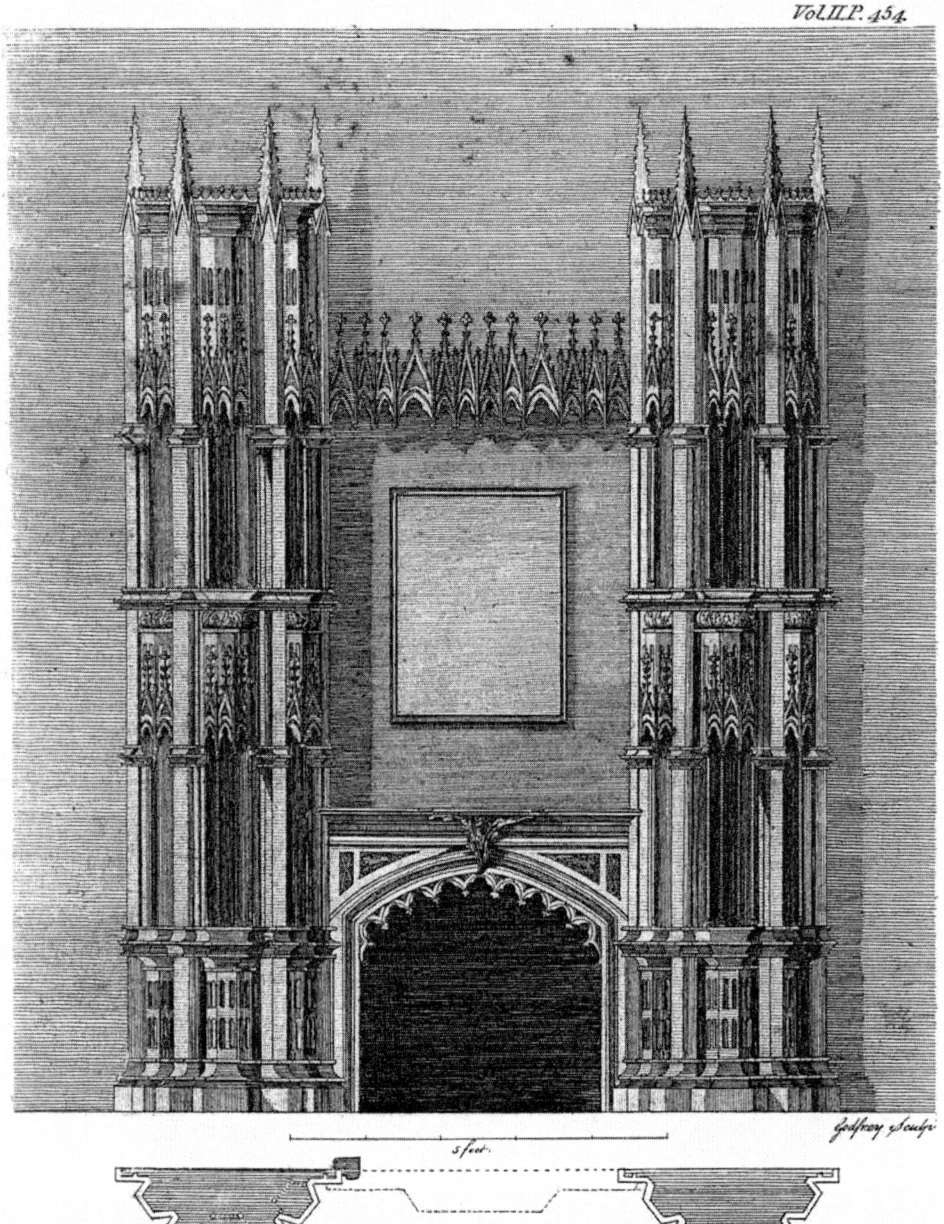

Chimney Piece of The Holbein Chamber.

combs: one of ivory is extremely ancient, carved with figures; on one ſide repreſenting perſons bathing and going to bed; on the other, two men and a woman with muſical inſtruments: another comb, ſaid to have belonged to the queen of Scots, is of tortoiſeſhell ſtudded with ſilver hearts and roſes; the two others of tortoiſeſhell likewiſe, of which the one with very long teeth belonged to the father of the firſt lord Edgcumbe, and was uſed when the large flowing wigs were in faſhion: two bottles of Roman fayence, and a baſon and ewer of purple and white Seve china.

A very ancient chair of oak, which came out of Glaſtonbury-abbey; on it are carved theſe ſentences, *Joannes Arthurus Monacus Glaſtonie, ſalvet eum Deus: Da pacem, Domine: Sit Laus Deo.* Lord Bathurſt had ſeveral chairs copied from this.

Another chair covered with purple cloth, made from one in a pane of painted glaſs in the breakfaſt-room.

The bed is of purple cloth lined with white ſatin, a plume of white and purple feathers on the centre of the teſter; the room is hung with purple paper. By the bed,

The red hat of cardinal Wolſey, found in the great wardrobe by biſhop Burnet when clerk of the cloſet. From his ſon the judge it came to the counteſs dowager of Albemarle, who gave it to Mr. Walpole.

Chriſt crowned with thorns, by Mabeuſe; bought at monſieur Hareng's ſale, 1764.

Over the chimney, an ancient painting of the emperor Maximilian and his ſon Philip the Fair: from the collection of Mr. Bryan Fairfax.

Lady Arabella Stuart, in white, whole length in water-colours; copied by Vertue from the original at Welbeck.

A man's head with a book; by Quintin Matſis: it was in ſir Robert Walpole's collection.

Anne Stanhope ducheſs of Somerſet, ſecond wife of the protector, whoſe portrait ſhe holds in one hand: a preſent to Mr. Walpole from Mr. Bateman.

Catherine

Catherine of Arragon †, firſt wife of Henry VIII. by Holbein: it was in the collection of ſir Robert Walpole, and has been engraved among the Illuſtrious Heads.

* Sir Thomas More. This and all the following heads marked with an aſteriſm, were taken off on oil-paper by Vertue from the original drawings of Holbein in queen Caroline's cloſet at Kenſington, now removed to Buckingham-houſe.

Lord Vaux. This is done in the ſame manner by Müntz, from the ſame collection.

A man's head, in old enamel.

Margaret queen of Navarre, who wrote the Tales: ditto.

Between the bow-windows:

Queen Elizabeth, when a girl.

* Lady Henningham.

* William Parr, marquis of Northampton, brother of queen Catherine Parr.

* A lady unknown.

* Ditto.

* Sir Nicholas Poines.

* Catherine Willoughby, fourth wife of Charles Brandon duke of Suffolk.

Queen Mary, when a child: from Mr. Fairfax's collection.

* Henry Howard earl of Surrey, the poet.

* Nicholas Cratzer, aſtronomer to Henry VIII.

† Vertue thought it to be Catherine ducheſs of Bar, ſiſter of Henry IV. of France, and ſo it probably is.

* Edward

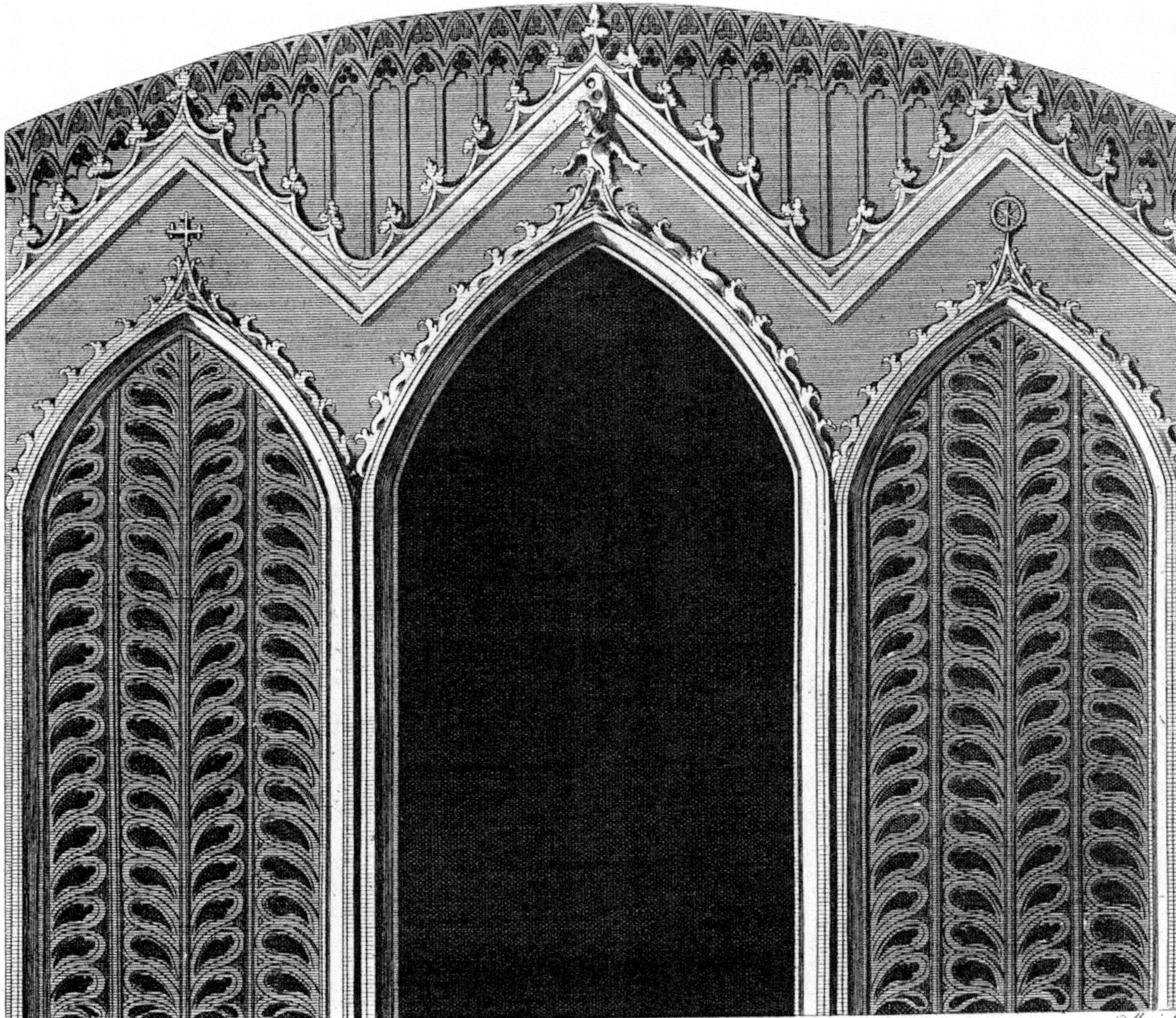

SCREEN OF THE HOLBEINCHAMBER.

* Edward Clinton earl of Lincoln, lord high admiral of England.

* Dr. Colet, dean of St. Paul's.

* Sir Thomas Elyot, the author.

* Henry Howard earl of Surrey; younger than the preceding.

Edmund Montacute, a judge; by Holbein: from ſir R. Walpole's collection.

* A gentleman, unknown.

* William Fitzwilliam earl of Southampton.

* Edward Stanley earl of Derby.

* Borbonius, a French poet.

* Fiſher biſhop of Rocheſter. Richardſon the painter had another of theſe, which was engraved among the Illuſtrious Heads.

* Thomas Boleyn earl of Ormond, father of queen Anne Boleyn.

On the ſide oppoſite to the chimney:

A fine and very valuable picture by Lucas de Heere, repreſenting Frances ducheſs of Suffolk, mother of the lady Jane Grey, and Adrian Stoke her ſecond huſband. This picture was in the collection of the earl of Oxford, and was engraved by Vertue. *Vide Anecdotes of Painting.*

Philip and Mary, copied in water-colours by Vertue, from the original by Antonio More, at the duke of Bedford's at Wooburn-abbey.

A ſingle combat before the emperor Maximilian, in terra cotta, by Albert Durer.

Anthony king of Navarre, father of Henry IV. by Janet.

The marechal de Montluc, who wrote the Commentaries: by ditto.

A very ſmall head of a man, in a round; by Holbein.

* Lord Wentworth.

* Lord chancellor Rich.

* Lady Rich, his wife.

* Sir Thomas Wyat, the poet.

* George Brook lord Cobham.

* Edward VI. when a child; very like Henry VIII.

* Jane Seymour.

Frobenius, the printer, in a round.
Melancthon, ditto; by Holbein; very fine. } Bought at sir W. Hamilton's sale, 1761.

A man's head with a black beard; ditto.

Margaret queen of Scots, daughter of Henry VII. copied by Vertue from the picture at Hampton-court.

Jane Gray; by ditto, from the original that was the duke of Somerset's.

Head of Henry VIII. with a watch at his neck, carved in box by Holbein.

* John Russel, first earl of Bedford.

* Anne Savage lady Berkeley. She held up the train of Anne Boleyn at her coronation: *Vide Stowe's Chron.* p. 543.

* Sir W. Sherrington, master of the mint, whence he furnished admiral Seymour with money.

* Sir John Gage.

* Sir Richard Southwell, one of the accusers of the earl of Surrey.

* Queen Mary, when princess.

* Thomas duke of Norfolk; beheaded in the reign of Elizabeth: young.

Holbein; in a round.
Anne Boleyn; ditto. } Copies by Eckardt.

Charlotte, daughter of Francis I. died at five years of age; by Janet: fine. From sir Luke Schaub's collection.

Lord Darnley, by Vertue, from the original at Hampton-court.

A young man's head; by Holbein.

Leonora, queen of Portugal, ſiſter of Charles V. and afterwards ſecond wife of Francis I.; by Vertue.

Henry VIII. fine whole figure in terra cotta, by Holbein; from lady Elizabeth Germaine's collection.

Pictures in the alcove:

The triumph of Riches; by Frederic Zucchero, from the original of Holbein that was in the Steel-yard. Henry VIII. in the character of Crœſus, and one of his queens, I believe Anne Boleyn, follow the car. *Vide a deſcription of this and the next in The Anecdotes of Painting.*

The triumph of Poverty; ditto. Theſe drawings, invaluable by the originals being loſt, were purchaſed from Buckingham-houſe when ſir Charles Sheffield ſold it to the king.

Arthur prince of Wales; a waſhed drawing, by E. Edwards, from the only original of that prince when grown up, which belonged to Mr. Sheldon of Weſton in Warwickſhire, and was purchaſed by Mr. Child of Oſterley-park, Middleſex, 1781.

A man's head with a red beard, in the manner of Holbein.

Richard III. by Vertue.

James V. and Mary of Lorraine his queen; in water-colours; by Wale; from an ancient original in the poſſeſſion of the duke of Devonſhire at Hardwicke.

Claude de Clermont ſieur de Dampier; by Janet.

Henry V. by Vertue.

Lord keeper Bacon; by Vertue.

John Howard, firſt duke of Norfolk, and his firſt wife Catherine, daughter of William lord Molins; two heads in rounds in one frame; copied by

 E. Edwards

E. Edwards in 1783 from the ancient originals, in oil on board, of the ſame ſize, in the poſſeſſion of the dowager lady Jerningham, to whom they came by deſcent, having been in the Arundelian collection. There is no other portrait of the duke, who was ſlain at Boſworth.

Mrs. Margaret Roper, daughter of ſir Thomas More; copied out of the great picture of the family, by Vertue.

Thomas lord Cromwell, in a round, after Holbein.

Head of ſir Thomas Wyat the younger, beheaded in the reign of queen Mary, in a round on board; copied by Milbourn, from the original in the poſſeſſion of lord Romney, who was related to the Wyats, and to whom the laſt bequeathed their portraits.

A man in black, by Holbein, in a rich gold frame; from the collection of H. Conſtantine Jennings, eſq. of Shiplake.

Over the door, Mary queen of Scots, a head; on her ruff, the arms of France and England.

A large drawing of a magnificent chimney-piece; a deſign by Holbein for one of the palaces of Henry VIII.

A man in black, holding a ring; ſmall half-length, by Holbein. On the back is written *H. II. data excel. Pnpis Valliſtari avunculi munere.*

A young lady, its companion; ſeems to be painted by Lionardo da Vinci. On the back, *Coſtanza Fregoſa, moglie del Co. Manfredo Lando, madre d'Agoſtino Landi Princ. di Val di Taro. Tableau du palais di Monaco. Pnpis Valliſtari munus.* Theſe two pictures were preſents to Mr. W. from his great nephew George earl of Cholmondeley.

Between the door and the ſcreen:

Henry VIII. three quarters; a preſent from the reverend Mr. Pennicott.

Henry duc de Longueville; in crayons.

Sir John Godſalve, knight of the carpet; after Holbein.

A drawing of architecture; by ditto.

Sir

Sir Thomas Wyat; by Vertue.

A man's head; an original drawing, by Holbein.

A man in a maſquerade habit; ditto.

Louis XI. an original: his prayer-book opens in the ſhape of a heart.

A drawing of a clock, by Holbein; deſigned for ſir Antony Denny as a new year's gift to Henry VIII. Bought at the ſale of Monſ. Mariette.

A drawing of a Romiſh epiſcopal ſaint; whole length, by Holbein.

A carpet worked by Mrs. Catherine Clive, the celebrated comedian.

The GALLERY.

FIFTY-SIX feet long, ſeventeen high, and thirteen wide without the five receſſes. The ceiling is taken from one of the ſide aiſles of Henry VIIth's chapel. In the windows, by Peckitt, are all the quarterings of the family. The great door is copied from the north door of ſaint Alban's, and the two ſmaller are parts of the ſame deſign. The ſide with receſſes, which are finiſhed with a gold net-work over looking-glaſs, is taken from the tomb of archbiſhop Bourchier at Canterbury. The chimney-piece was deſigned by Mr. John Chute, and Mr. Thomas Pitt of Boconnoch. The room is hung with crimſon Norwich damaſk: the chairs, ſettees, and long ſtools are of the ſame, mounted on black and gold frames. The carpet made at Moorfields.

East end:

Laura and Charlotte Walpole, eldeſt and youngeſt daughters of ſir Edward Walpole, and wives of Frederic Keppel biſhop of Exeter, and of Lionel Talmach earl of Dyſart; Mrs. Keppel in white, lady Dyſart in pink: by Ramſay.

Marriage of Henry VII. and Elizabeth of York; by Mabeuſe. *Vide Anecdotes of Painting.*

Sir Francis Walſingham, with a view of his houſe at Scadbury in Kent; by Frederic Zucchero: from ſir Robert Walpole's collection. This picture has been engraved by Houbraken amongſt the Illuſtrious Heads.

Sir George Villiers, leaning his hand on the head of a greyhound. He was father of George duke of Buckingham, and lord Clarendon relates a ſtory of his ghoſt. This is a very fine picture: by Cornelius Janſen.

George duke of Buckingham, his ſon: a very fine head, by Rubens: the garter is put on the wrong way.

Admiral Montagu earl of Sandwich; by ſir Peter Lely: very good head. Lord Sandwich gave this to Mr. Blackwood, from whom Mr. Walpole bought it.

Holy family, with boy angels, in a landſcape; by Van Artois, ſcholar of Rubens: from ſir Robert Walpole's collection.

Inſide of an ancient Flemiſh houſe; by old Frank.

A cheſt * of old japan inlaid with mother of pearl.

Two coins of old japan with marble ſlabs. On one,

A bronze of the Hercules Farneſe.

A light blue pot pourri of Seve, mounted in or moulu:

Two octagon baſons, Saxon, old china pattern.

On the other, a buſt of Tiberius; bought at Mr. Jennings's ſale: another pot pourri; and two Saxon baſons.

Chimney-ſide, left hand:

On the hearth, two tubs of old blue and white porcelaine; a preſent from Mrs. Goſtling.

Virgin and child, after the picture of Dominichino, at Houghton; by John Davis, eſq. of Watlington.

* In this cheſt are three ſlaſhed doublets, a cloak ditto, and a pair of black embroidered breeches, which belonged to Robert Walpole, great grandfather of ſir Robert Walpole firſt earl of Orford, and had been preſerved in the old houſe at Houghton: given by George lord Orford.

Mr.

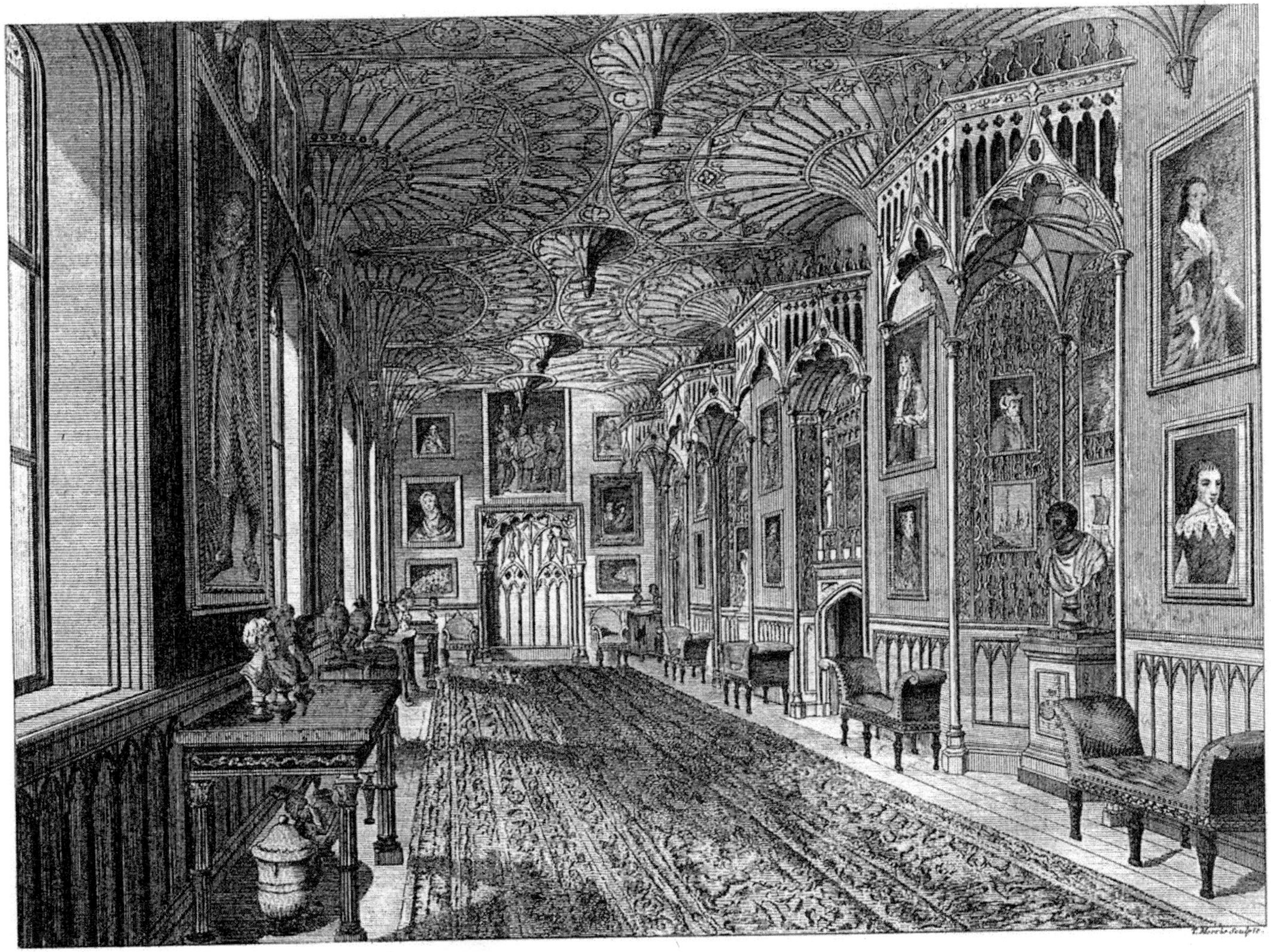

THE GALLERY

Mr. Leneve, maſter of the company of merchant taylors: a moſt bright and pure picture, by Cornelius Janſen.

Marguerite de Valois, ducheſſe de Savoie, ſiſter of Henry II. of France; he was killed at the tournament for her wedding: by ſir Antonio More. This picture belonged to king Charles I. In one niche,

Maria, ſecond daughter of ſir Edward Walpole, widow of James earl of Waldegrave, and wife of William Henry duke of Glouceſter, brother of king George III. by ſir Joſhua Reynolds.

John Law, inventor of the Miſſiſippi-ſcheme, and prime miniſter to the regent Philip duke of Orleans: one of the beſt of Roſalba's works.

Francis Seymour Conway earl of Hertford; by ditto.

Death of Admiral Sandwich; by Scott.

Views, of Kirkſtall-abbey, and of a church near Boulogne in France; by ditto.

The eagle found in the gardens of Boccapadugli within the precinct of Caracalla's baths at Rome, in the year 1742. One of the fineſt pieces of Greek ſculpture in the world, and reckoned ſuperior to the eagle in the villa Mattei. There are extremely few fine ſtatues of animals; the chief are theſe two eagles, the Tuſcan boar, the Barberini goat, and the dog belonging to Mr. Jennings of Shiplake *. The boldneſs, and yet great finiſhing of this ſtatue, are incomparable; the eyes inimitable. Mr. Gray has drawn *the flagging wing* †. It ſtands on a handſome antique ſepulchral altar, adorned with eagles too.

Frances Bridges, daughter of the lord Chandos, and ſecond wife of Thomas Cecil earl of Exeter, on whoſe left hand ſhe refuſed to lie on his tomb in Weſtminſter-abbey. This picture, which is an excellent one of Vandyck, belonged to Richardſon the painter, who has written a diſſertation of eight pages on it in one of his books ‡. It was purchaſed of Hudſon the painter, ſon-in-law of Richardſon.

* Since bought by Mr. Duncombe.

† Ode on the Power of Poetry.

‡ This lady was moſt falſely accuſed of many crimes, of which ſhe was entirely innocent, and acquitted; of which ſee an account in Granger's Biographical Hiſtory of Engliſh Portraits, vol. i. p. 548.

A young

A young man; by ſir Godfrey Kneller: quære, if not his own portrait? From the collection of Sclater Bacon of Cambridgeſhire.

Over a door, Catherine Sidley counteſs of Dorcheſter, miſtreſs of James II. and mother of the ducheſs of Buckingham; by Dahl.

Madame de Sevigné; a head: a preſent from lady Hervey.

A girl ſcouring pots; a curious picture, being painted by Watteau in the ſtyle of Rembrandt. It was in the collection of Mr. Cooke member for Middleſex.

A landſcape by Müntz, painted in encauſtic, which he improved from count Caylus's rules.

Thomas earl of Arundel, and his grandſon cardinal Howard; in water-colours, by Vertue, after Vandyck.

Right hand of the chimney:

—— Leneve, alderman of Norwich; ſon of the foregoing Leneve. The beſt picture ſir Peter Lely ever painted, and as fine as Vandyck's counteſs of Exeter, before mentioned.

His wife, in blue; ditto.

John lord Sheffield, huſband of lady Douglas Sheffield, on whoſe account it was ſurmiſed that he was poiſoned by R. earl of Leiceſter; by Ant. More: from Buckingham-houſe.

Henry Jermyn earl of ſaint Albans, favourite, and, as ſir John Rereſby ſays, ſecond huſband of queen Henrietta Maria: probably by Old Stone.

James II. earl of Waldegrave; by Reynolds.

Bacha Bonneval; by Liotard: bought at the ſale of Everard Falkner, knt. embaſſador to the Porte.

Henry Fox lord Holland; by ditto.

Sea-piece; views, of Briſtol-croſs, and of a Gothic farm near Marble-hill,

hill, belonging to the countefs of Suffolk, and defigned by Richard Bentley: all by Sam. Scott.

Vefpafian, in bafaltes; a noble buft, bought out of the collection of cardinal Ottoboni. It ftands on a Roman fepulchral altar, on which, in bas-relief, is a man facrificing, with this infcription,

TI. CLAVDIVS AVG. L.
DOCILIS
AEDITVS AEDIS
FORTVNAE TVLLIANAE.

Over a door, Anne Hyde duchefs of York; by Mrs. Beale, after fir Peter Lely.

Lady Sophia Farmor, eldeft daughter of Thomas earl of Pomfret, and fecond wife of John earl Granville, prime minifter to George II.: by Rofalba. She is drawn as Juno.

Two men cheating another at cards; by John Miel: very good.

A landfcape in encauftic; by Müntz.

West end:

A large piece of Catherine de' Medici and her children, Charles IX. Henry III. the duke d'Alençon, and Margaret queen of Navarre; whole lengths, by Janet: bought from Mr. Byde's in Hertfordfhire.

Griffiere, the painter; by Zouft: the fatin on the arm remarkably well painted.

A young man's head, æt. 18; admirable nature: by Giorgione. This was in the collection of Charles I. *Vide Topham's Catalogue.*

A pot of flowers, highly finifhed, yet very free; by old Baptift. From fir Robert Walpole's collection.

Sevonyans the painter, by himfelf; a very fine head.

Charles Brandon duke of Suffolk, and Mary queen of France. This picture was lord Granville's. Kent defigned the frame. The picture had before been at the earl of Weftmorland's at Apthorpe.

 Tobit

Tobit burying the dead. *And when Tob t found any dead, he buried them without the walls of Jerusalem:* by Benedetto Castiglione.

A coin of old Japan; on it, busts of Julia Domna, Julia Titi, and Cicero; the latter a present from lady Hervey; a flat vase of white, blue and gold Seve china, with cover and handles.

Another coin, ditto; statue of Harpocrates and Telesphorus; Antinous, Greek work; and Zenocrates, a present from general Conway; a flat vase, like the former.

Window side:

Thomas lord Howard of Bindon, father of Frances duchess of Richmond and Lenox; whole length, in robes of the garter.

Lodowic Stuart duke of Richmond and Lenox; ditto: these two last came out of Luton-house in Bedfordshire, where the latter lived.

Frances duchess of Richmond and Lenox. *See a curious account of this great lady in Wilson's Reign of king James the first.* This picture came from Easton-Neston, the seat of Thomas earl of Pomfret. By Mark Garrard.

Henry Carey lord Falkland, deputy of Ireland, and father of the famous Lucius lord Falkland; in white *, by Vansomer.

Mrs. Catharine Philips, the poetess; a head: it belonged to Charles earl of Halifax.

Philip Villiers de Lisle Adam, the last grand-master of Rhodes, which he defended two years against Solyman the Magnificent and a prodigious army: a head.

A view of mount Orgueil in Jersey; by Richard Bentley, esq.

Heads in the upper line, begin from the left:

Vandyck. Richard Rigby, paymaster of the forces and master of the rolls in Ireland, by Eckardt. Prior, the poet. Cooke, the painter; by himself. General Edward Cornwallis, governor of Gibraltar and groom of the bedchamber to George II. by Eckardt. Pearce, senior, statuary. Waller,

* The idea of the picture walking out of its frame in The Castle of Otranto, was suggested by this portrait.

the

the poet. Horatio lord Walpole, younger brother of ſir Robert Walpole; by Vanloo. Mr. Chiffinch, privy-purſe to Charles II. by Riley. Dobſon, the painter. George Keppel, third earl of Albemarle; by Eckardt. Sir Nicholas Dorigny, the engraver. Van Wyck, the younger, painter. George Montagu, eſq. by Eckardt, after Vanloo. Dahl, the painter.

Anne Clifford *, counteſs of Dorſet, Pembroke and Montgomery. There is a medal of her taken exactly from this picture.

Thomas Howard duke of Norfolk, beheaded for the cauſe of the queen of Scots. In this picture he is young, and it was probably painted in the reign of Edward VI. before he was reſtored in blood; for there are his arms without a coronet, and yet on his handkerchief are an N and a †, to mark his title and his religion: by Antonio More.

A ſea-piece, by Scott.

A fine ſmall landſcape with ſheep, by Gaſpar Pouſſin; a legacy from ſir Horace Mann, envoy to Florence.

Bronzes in the windows; an ‡ Ibis: a Ceres with ſilver eyes, and a cow in her lap: the Laocoon: Antinous ‡ on a tripod: an oſtrich, very ſpirited.

Two tables of ſolid granite, from the Farneſe gardens at Rome; the frames black and gold, from a tomb in Weſtminſter-abbey.

On the firſt table, buſts of Marcus Aurelius: Domitilla, wife of Veſpaſian, exceedingly rare: a Camillus or ſacrificing prieſt. Beneath, a bronze from John of Boulogne's Rape of the Sabines: two antique urns of marble; that with a cover heavily deſigned by Kent belonged to Brian Fairfax.

On the other table, buſts of Julia Mœſa: Fauſtina ſenior: and Antonia Claudii Mater: very rare. Beneath, the liſtening ſlave in bronze: and two antique urns of marble: on one this inſcription, PAILIOVI RITIO FILIO SVO QVI BISIT ANNIS XX FECIT SIBI.

Two commodes of old Japan with marble ſlabs; on one, a triangular ciſtern of Roman fayence, finely painted with figures, probably from deſigns

* See an account of her in the Catalogue of Royal and Noble Authors.

‡ From Dr. Middleton's collection.

of Julio Romano; two large vaſes, ditto, finely painted, and inſcribed, FATTE IN BOTEGA DE ORATIO FONTANA, and mounted in or moulu.

On the other commode, another ciſtern * like the former; and two bottles of blue and white and gold Seve china, moſt beautifully deſigned and ornamented.

A mother of pearl box, with fiſhes and counters of the ſame; a preſent from Mrs. Clive.

In a CLOSET, with glaſs doors, between the gallery and round chamber, is a large collection of ancient porcelaine of China, which belonged to Catherine lady Walpole. Under the window, a ſmall altar, part of the ſhrine in the chapel, and on it a ſilver ladle with an ivory handle carved and gilt, uſed by Indian ladies for incenſe; a preſent from Charles duke of Richmond.

Three blue baſkets made like ruſhes, of old blue china; bought at the ſale of the ducheſs dowager of Portland.

THE ROUND DRAWING-ROOM.

HUNG with crimſon Norwick damaſk: the chairs of Aubuſſon tapeſtry, flowers on a white ground, the frames green and gold; and a carpet of the manufacture of Moorfields; the deſign taken from the Seve china-table in the Green Cloſet.

The deſign of the chimney-piece is taken from the tomb of Edward the Confeſſor, improved by Mr. Adam, and beautifully executed in white marble inlaid with ſcagliuola, by Richter. The dogs are ſilver: on the chimney are three large jars and two beakers, of ſilver alſo, bought at the auction of lady Eliz. Germaine; on the middle one is the Rape of the Sabines emboſſed. Two ſilver ſconces, with hiſtories, on the ſides.

A ſcreen worked in chenille, to ſuit with the chimney, by the counteſs of Aileſbury.

* Preſents from the earl of Exeter; and had belonged to Jervas the painter, who had a fine collection of that fayence.

The

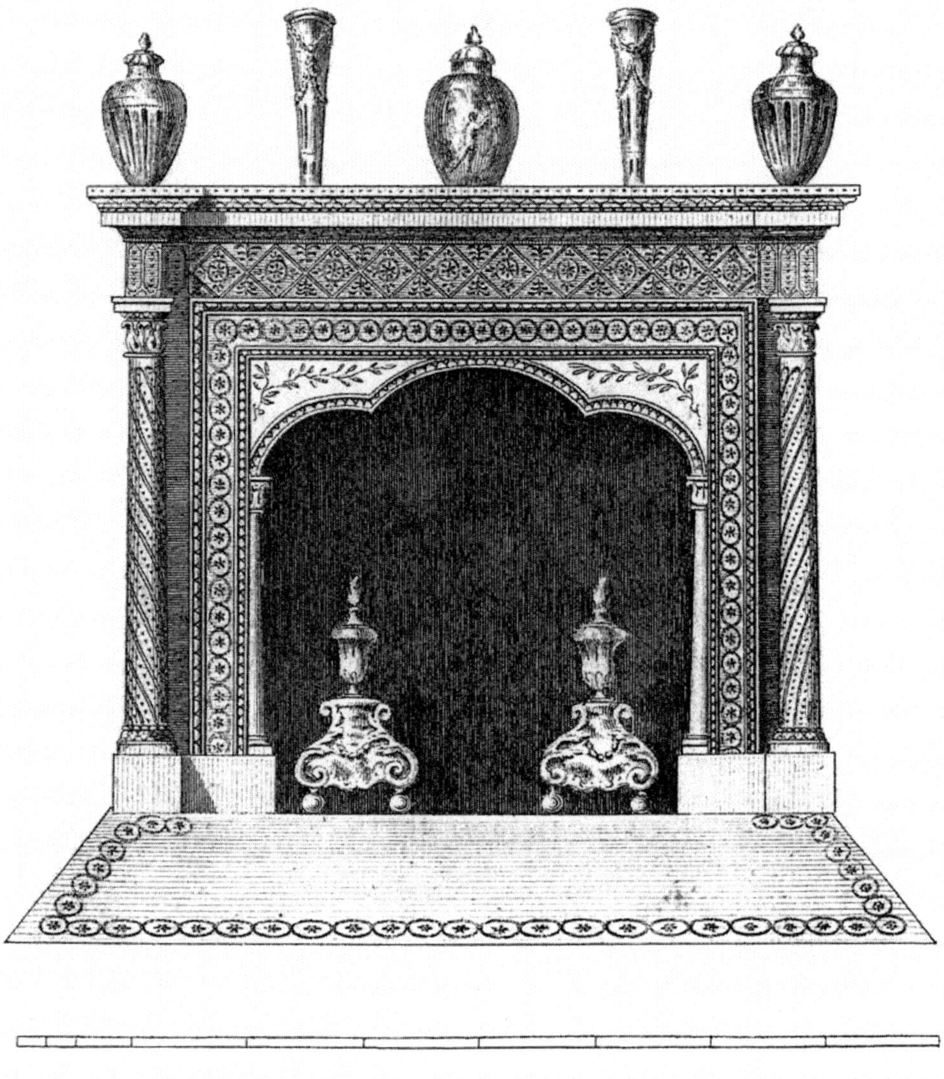

CHIMNEY IN THE ROUND ROOM

The ceiling is taken from a round window in old Saint Paul's; the frieze was designed by Mr. Adam.

In the great bow window is a large shield of the arms of Robert Dudley earl of Leicester, given by Mr. H. Reade; under it a thornbush with H R, the device of Henry VII.; the arms of queen Elizabeth, on the left hand, from Essex-house in the Strand; roses; other arms of nobility; and six fine pieces, by a scholar of Price, from Raphael's bible. The surbase of the window is taken from the tomb of queen Eleanor in Westminster-abbey.

Over the chimney, lady Dorothy Percy countess of Leicester, in red, and her sister lady Lucy, the famous countess of Carlisle; a very capital picture of Vandyck, sold out of Penshurst by lady Yonge, when she inherited half of that ancient seat by the will of lady Brownlow. Mr. Hoare of Stourhead offered the last earl of Leicester of the Sidney family an hundred pounds for this picture.

Over the door, Mrs. Lemon, mistress of Vandyck, with a sword, as Judith; by Vandyck; bought out of Buckingham-house: very boldly and freely painted.

Bianca Capello; by Vasari; bought out of the Vitelli palace at Florence by sir Horace Mann, and sent to Mr. Walpole: the hands never finished. Her story is thus written in a cartouche on the frame: *Bianca Capello, a Venetian lady, who having disobliged her family by marrying a Florentine banker, was reduced to maintain him by washing linen; Francis the great-duke saw, fell in love with, and made her his mistress, and her husband his minister: but the latter, after numberless tyrannies, for which she obtained his pardon, and after repeated ill usage of her, for which she pardoned him, having murdered a man, and being again protected by her, the great-duke told her, that, though he would remit her husband's punishment, he would pardon whoever should kill him. The relations of the deceased murdered the assassin, and Francis married his widow Bianca, who was poisoned with him at a banquet by cardinal Ferdinand, afterwards called the Great, brother and successor of duke Francis* *.

* Montaigne, in his Travels, vol. i. p. 251, gives a description of Bianca, which corresponds much with this portrait. "Cette duchesse est belle à l'opinion Italienne, un visage agreable et imperieux, le corsage gros, et de tetins à leur souhait." The small portrait of her in the cabinet of enamels here, p. 475, is younger and much handsomer.

Jacob

Jacob travelling from Laban; very fine; by Salvator Rosa. A present from sir Horace Mann.

The education of Jupiter; by Nicolo Poussin. This picture cost sir Robert Walpole an hundred and fourteen pounds.

A most beautiful landscape by Paul Brill.

A piece of rocks, with the temple of Tivoli; by Gobbo Caracci.

A trunk of tortoiseshell and bronze; by Boul, on a frame of the same. A small jar of Seve china under it.

A japan cabinet. On it, two double branched silver candlesticks with figures of women, bought at lady Vere's sale in 1783; and a bronze figure of Moses, after Michael Angelo. Under it, a large vase of Florentine fayence, with the arms of the great-duke.

Two old japan coffers on gilt frames. Under them, two large bottles of Florentine fayence, with the arms of duke Ferdinand of Medici and his wife Christina of Lorraine.

In the window, a green and gold table and two high stands, with the cyphers of sir Robert Walpole and Catharine Shorter his first wife. On the table, two vases, boat-shaped, of deep blue Seve china, mounted in or moulu, with snake handles. Beneath a large round vase and cover, and a dish to it, of Roman fayence.

The TRIBUNE.

IT is a square with a semicircular recess in the middle of each side, painted stone-colour with gilt ornaments, and with windows and niches, the latter taken from those on the sides of the north door of the great church at Saint Alban's: the roof, which is taken from the chapter-house at York, is terminated by a star of yellow glass that throws a golden gloom all over the room, and with the painted windows gives it the solemn air of a rich chapel. The windows contain a head of Christ and two apostles, one in the middle of each, set round with four histories, all old, but finely re-coloured by Price, and surrounded with most beautiful mosaics of the purest taste. In five of the niches, on pedestals, are,

1. A cast in plaister bronzed of Catherine lady Walpole, the model of

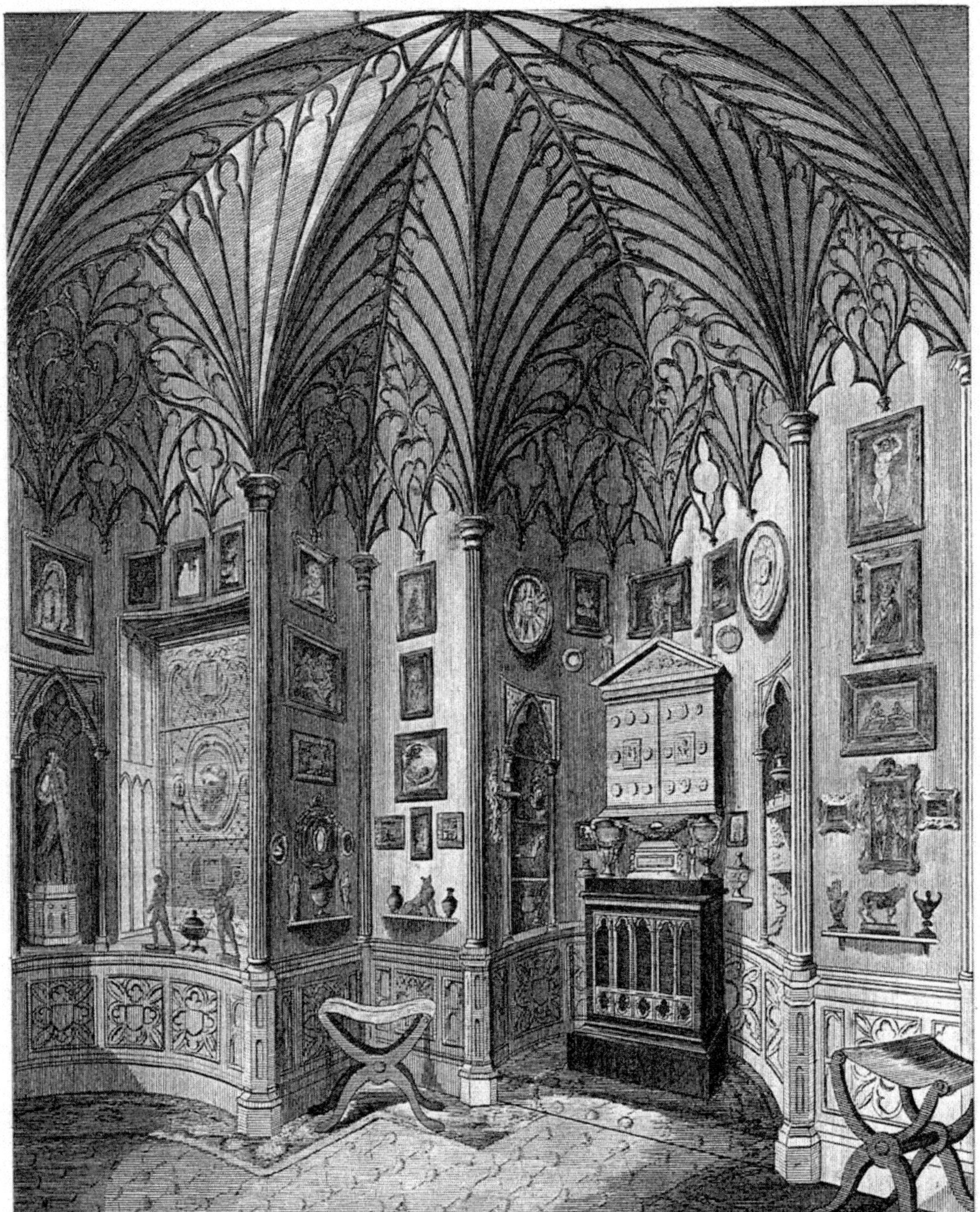

T. Morris sc.

THE CABINET

her ſtatue in Weſtminſter-abbey, executed at Rome by Valory, and taken from the Livia or Pudicitia in the villa Mattei. 2. The Venus * of Medici. 3. Antinous. 4. The Apollo Belvedere. 5. The Farneſe Flora in bronze. In the windows, ſix ſmaller bronzes from ancient ſtatues ; a Chineſe incenſe-box of bronze ; and two pots-pourris of red japan ſet in or moulu and ſurmounted with Indian figures by Martin. The carpet is taken from the moſaic of the windows, and in the middle has the reflection from the ſtar in the ceiling. The grated door was deſigned by Mr. Thomas Pitt.

On the right hand ſtands an altar of black and gold, with a marble ſlab of the ſame colours, taken from the tomb of two children of Edward III. in Weſtminſter-abbey. On the altar, a Florentine box inlaid with hard ſtones, a preſent from ſir Horace Mann : two moſt beautiful vaſes in paſte, imitating root of amethyſt and ornamented with vines and heads of goats, by Germaine of Paris : a ſilver diſh of baſket-work, and two candleſticks of German agate, preſents from General H. S. Conway. On the ſides, two ſilver ſconces with the arms of Frances Pelham † viſcounteſs Caſtlecomer ; and two vaſes of ivory from the antique, carved by Verſkovis. Over the altar,

A cabinet of roſe-wood, deſigned by Mr. Walpole ; on the pediment, ſtatues in ivory of Fiamingo, Inigo Jones and Palladio, by Verſkovis, after the models of Ryſbrack. In the pediment, Mr. Walpole's arms, a Cupid and lion, by the ſame : on the doors, bas-reliefs in ivory, Herodias with the head of the Baptiſt, by Gibbons; a lady, half-length, by the ſame ; Perſeus and Andromeda ; the Hercules Farneſe ; the Flora ; Diomede with the Palladium ; the Meduſa of Strozzi ; the Perſeus of ditto ; Caracalla and Alexander, by Pozzo ; and eight other heads. On the drawer, the Barberini lion, by Pozzo ; and heads of eagles, by Verſkovis.

Within the cabinet of enamels and miniatures :

The virgin and child, in miniature, round ; by Old Lens, from the original by Annibal Caracci, at Kenſington.

Head of Chriſt ; by Carlo Dolce ; in a rich frame of ſilver gilt ; and ſilver cherubim.

* The Venus and Antinous were lord Waldegrave's.

† Siſter of Thomas duke of Newcaſtle ; ſhe died and is buried at Twickenham.

Venus,

Venus, Cupid, and other figures in enamel; by Boit, from the original by Luca Giordano, at Devonſhire-houſe.

Ethelreda Harriſon, wife of Charles viſcount Townſhend; a capital piece of enamel, by Zincke, after Vanloo; ſet in a frame of enamel flowers in relief; on the back, her arms ſupported by Cupids, enamelled by Groth.

A fine old enamelled watch-caſe, after Raphael and Dominichino.

Emperor Joſeph I. ſmall.

Colonel Horatio Walpole, uncle of ſir Robert Walpole; ſmall.

The ducheſſes of Cleveland and Portſmouth; very ſmall.

Sir Edward Walpole, father of Maria ducheſs of Glouceſter, in enamel; by Zincke.

Galfridus Walpole, youngeſt brother of ſir Robert Walpole; in water-colours.

Byzas, imaginary founder of Byzantium; large intaglia on onyx. M.*

A valuable jewel of lord Burleigh's head on onyx, by Valerio Vicentino, cut on the reverſe of an antique of Caracalla; appendent is the head of queen Elizabeth, cut likewiſe on ſardonyx, by the ſame Vicentino; the whole ſet with 53 brilliants, given to Mr. Walpole by his father, who bought it of ſir Andrew Fountaine, who had it ſet on purpoſe, with alluſion to queen Caroline and ſir Robert Walpole.

Sir Robert Walpole earl of Orford; very like; painted in enamel by Zincke, two years before ſir Robert's death: ſet in a frame of enamelled oak-leaves.

Catherine Shorter, firſt wife of ſir Robert Walpole; ditto, after ſir Godfrey Kneller: ſet with enamel flowers. The two heads are in Zincke's beſt manner, and were engraved for the Ædes Walpolianæ.

Mary Walpole, ſecond daughter of ſir Robert Walpole and Catherine

* All the curioſities marked M. belonged to Dr. Conyers Middleton, whoſe whole collection Mr. Walpole bought. See an account of them in the doctor's Germana quædam Antiquitatis Monumenta.

Shorter,

Shorter, and wife of George Cholmondeley viſcount Malpas, afterwards earl of Cholmondeley; in water-colours; by Groth, after Jervas.

Lady Maria Walpole, only child of ſir Robert Walpole and Maria Skerret his ſecond wife, married to Charles Churchill, eſq. in enamel; by Zincke.

Horace Walpole, [who made the collection] youngeſt ſon of ſir R. Walpole and Catherine Shorter; ditto.

Horatio Walpole lord Walpole, brother of ſir Robert; in enamel; by Groth, after Vanloo.

Two lockets in ſhape of hearts, with hair of ſir Robert Walpole and Catherine Shorter, ſet with diamonds.

An Egyptian duck; antique cameo, on agate. M.

A ſleeping hermaphrodite with two ſatyrs; ditto: very fine. M.

Sir Anthony Shirley, embaſſador *from* the ſophy of Perſia *to* king James the firſt; dreſs, half Engliſh half Perſian: by Iſaac Oliver.

The queen of Bohemia; by Iſaac Oliver: bought out of the collection of lady Iſabella Scott, daughter of the ducheſs of Monmouth.

Serjeant Maynard; by Hoſkins: given to ſir R. Walpole by ſir Everard Falkener.

Sir Kenelm Digby; by Peter Oliver: it was in doctor Meade's collection.

James I. by Iſaac Oliver.

Charles I. by Petitot: fine. A preſent from T. Walker, eſq. to Maria lady Walpole.

Charles II. ditto; in a caſe enamelled blue; done abroad: bought of an old gentlewoman to whom he gave it when he ſtood godfather to her in Holland.

James II. when duke of York; fine, by Petitot: bought at the ſale of Mrs. Dunch, daughter of his miſtreſs, Mrs. Godfrey.

Robert Cecil earl of Saliſbury; by Iſaac Oliver.

A lady's head, in enamel; by Petitot.

Nicholas Burwell, brother of ſir Jeffery Burwell, grandfather of ſir Robert Walpole; by Hoſkins: ſet in a caſe with ſmall diamonds, and enamelled with The judgment of Paris in relief: very neat.

Mrs. Godfrey, miſtreſs of king James, in enamel; by Petitot: was Mrs. Dunch's, her daughter.

Robert Devereux earl of Eſſex; by Iſaac Oliver: it belonged to Frances lady Worſeley, who was deſcended from him. It was engraved for the Illuſtrious Heads.

Frances his wife, daughter of ſir Francis Walſingham, widow of ſir Philip Sidney, and laſtly wife of the earl of Clanrickard and Saint Albans.

Robert Walpole, ſecond earl of Orford; painted in water-colours by Roſalba with all the force of oil.

An elderly lady's head, by Cooper; fine.

Robert Carr earl of Somerſet, in his latter time, favourite of king James; by Hoſkins: bought at the ſale of the curious collection of T. Barrett, of Lees in Kent, 1758.

Richard Cromwell, protector, in armour; by Cooper: from the ſame collection.

Marivaux, author of Marianne; by Liotard; in water-colours.

George Walpole, third earl of Orford; ditto.

John Chute, eſq. of the Vine in Hampſhire; finely painted in water-colours, by Pompeio Battoni, at Rome.

A watch enamelled with hiſtories, after Pietro Cortona.

Another enamelled watch.

Admiral Churchill, brother of John duke of Marlborough; very finely enamelled by Boit: it belonged to his niece, Mrs. Dunch.

A curious

A curious antique miniature in gold, of a Roman lady and her ſon; the boy has a bulla at his neck. M.

Lady Arabella Stuart; by Hilliard: it was lord Wilmington's.

Queen Elizabeth; ditto; ditto.

George II. by Mr. Deacon.

Cowley, the poet, after ſir Peter Lely; by Zincke: his maſter-piece, and perhaps the fineſt piece of enamel in the world. It was engraved for Mr. Hurd's edition of Cowley.

A lady, ſaid to be Henrietta ducheſs of Orleans, but probably Martinozzi, princeſs of Conti: one of the fineſt works of Petitot. A looking-glaſs behind it: bought of Zincke.

A beautiful enamel, by Petitot, of Catherine Henriette d'Angennes comteſſe d'Olonne, as a Diana, a character very different from that given of her in Buſſy's Hiſtoire amoureuſe des Gaules. It is ſet in a frame of flowers enamelled in relief by Giles Legaré de Chaumont en Baſſigni, who was famous for that ſort of works: from the collection of Monſieur Mariette.

Bianca Capello, great ducheſs of Tuſcany; a ſmall head in oil, by Bronzino. *See her hiſtory, p. 469.*

Louis XIV: Mary of Auſtria, his queen: Anne of Auſtria, his mother, very delicate: madame de Monteſpan, his miſtreſs, beautiful. Theſe four are ſmall heads in enamel, by Petitot.

Mrs. Middleton, a beauty in the reign of Charles II. ditto; by ditto.

Ducheſs of Mazarin, in water-colours.

Conſtant Hayes, wife of Galfridus Walpole, and afterwards of Mr. Kerwood; very ſmall.

A ſilver gilt heart; within, the arms of ſir Robert and Catherine lady Walpole: his firſt preſent to her on their marriage.

Anne Boleyn; copied by Wale from a portrait of her by Hoſkins, which he did from an ancient picture of her for king Charles I. and which is mentioned

mentioned in his catalogue with other royal miniatures in the ſame frame; all which are now in the poſſeſſion of the duke of Richmond.

Catherine Parr, by Holbein; a moſt ſcarce head, and exactly like the picture of her at the earl of Denbigh's at Nuneham Padox, Warwickſhire.

A girl with flowers, in water-colours; by Roſalba.

Oliver Cromwell; by Boit, after Cooper: given to Mr. Walpole by his brother lord Orford.

John Dodd, of Swallowfield, Bucks; by Rouquet.

Catherine Clopton, wife of Henry Talbot, and couſin of Catherine lady Walpole; by Zincke.

Jane Seymour; by Holbein, in water-colours: was lady Worſeley's.

Peter Oliver, profile in black lead, from a leaf of his own pocket-book, and his wife, full-faced, on the other ſide; both fine: it belonged to Vertue the engraver.

Lucius Carey, the famous lord Falkland; by Hoſkins; fine: it was Dr. Meade's.

Doctor Bragge, a dealer in pictures; by Mr. J. Deacon.

A calcedonian ſtone; antique, uſed as an ornament to a horſe of a triumphal chariot. M.

Another ſtone; deſcribed in Germana quædam. M.

On the inſides of the doors:

Thomas Howard duke of Norfolk, beheaded temp. Elizabeth; by Antonio More: belonged to Richardſon the painter, and engraved among the Illuſtrious Heads.

A lady, painted by Holbein; engraved by Hollar when in the Arundelian collection, and probably Mary Tudor queen of France, ſiſter of Henry VIII. but amongſt the Illuſtrious Heads called Catherine Howard. This alſo was Richardſon's.

Lucy

Lucy Barlow, alias Waters, mother of the duke of Monmouth; by Cooper.

Catherine of Arragon, first wife of Henry VIII. an admirable original; by Holbein. These two were bought at the auction of lady Isabella Scott.

A young man in black; copied by lady Lucan from a portrait by Titian, in the collection of the duke of Devonshire.

A lady's head, by Rosalba; set in tortoiseshell.

James Brydges, first duke of Chandos; in enamel, by Zincke: a present from G. S. earl of Harcourt.

A golden heart set with jewels, and ornamented with emblematic figures enamelled, and Scottish mottos; made by order of the lady Margaret Douglas, mother of Henry lord Darnley, in memory of her husband Matthew Stuart earl of Lenox and regent of Scotland, murdered by the papists.

Isaac Oliver, by himself; perfectly fine.

Waller, the poet; by Cooper: and a lord Digby; ditto. These three from the collection of Mr. Barrett of Lees.

Liotard the painter, in his Turkish dress, in enamel, by himself; given to Mr. Walpole by his sister lady Mary Churchill.

Salmacis and Hermaphroditus, a most beautiful miniature by Clinksted; given to Mr. Walpole by Mr. Chute: set in a gold frame enamelled blue.

A naked Venus, whole length, and very fine; the attitude copied by Zincke from a picture of Annibal Caracci in the collection at Houghton: set in a frame like the former.

A small head of a foreign general, in buff with a black sash. It is painted with all the force of oil, though in enamel, and in a grander style than Petitot's. From the Portland collection.

Hair of king Edward IV. cut from his corpse when discovered in St. George's chapel at Windsor, 1789; given by sir Joseph Banks. [*End of the cabinet of enamels and miniatures.*

Other

Other pictures and curiosities in the same room :

Little children presented to Christ ; Italian, on copper.

The virgin, child, and saint John ; Baroccio, after Correggio.

The virgin and child, by Carlo Cignani ; from lord Cholmondeley's collection.

Head of a cardinal ; and an old man's head ; rounds, on fayence.

A fine dish, enamelled on copper, with the history of Moses. P. R. 1557.

A fayence dish, painted in grotesque.

Rembrandt ; by old Lens.

Lady Mary Wortley Montagu, as a shepherdess ; after Jervas ; by ditto.

Two vases carved in ivory, by Verskovis, after the antique.

Queen Anne of Denmark ; and a lady of the same time ; by Isaac Oliver : in one frame.

Louis XII. of France ; and sir John Gage ; by Holbein : in another frame. These from the collection of lady Elizabeth Germaine.

Margaret of Austria, daughter of Charles V. in a white religious habit ; enamelled on copper, in a round : behind it, Moses receiving the law ; enamelled on gold.

Louis XII. in enamel. These two were presents to Mr. Walpole from miss Rachael Lloyd, and belonged to the princess Sophia, mother of king George I.

Lord Loudon, chancellor of Scotland ; by Samuel Cooper.

In the glass-case near the window :

A chalice of silver gilt, richly ornamented with figures, jewels and crystal.

Model of the shrine of Thomas Becket, enamelled.

An amber jewel-box.

Great ſeal of Theodore king of Corſica.

That very curious piece by which he took the benefit of the act of inſolvency: he is only ſtyled, Theodore Stephen baron de Newhoff.

His capitulations made with the people of Corſica, on his election, ſigned by his own hand.

An antique figure of the deity of gardens; fine.

Two phalli, a fibula, two ſacrificing inſtruments, and a ſmall eagle; all of bronze. M.

Gold medal of Maximilian, with a chain enamelled.

A croſs of cedar inlaid with mother of pearl.

A ſmall gold watch, given by George II. when prince of Wales to Catherine lady Walpole.

An ancient ſquare German watch, curiouſly chaſed in ſilver gilt.

A coffer enamelled on all ſides with battles, and ſet in ſilver gilt.

Two caudle-cups, with flowers on gold grounds, of Chelſea porcelaine.

A red ſnuff-box, with enamelled top and bottom; given to Mr. Walpole by Francis earl of Hertford.

A ſquare ſnuff-box of lapis-lazuli, ſet in gold.

A round ſnuff-box of ditto, ſet in gold enamelled.

A ſmall buſt of Veſpaſian in cornelian.

An agate cup and ſaucer.

A ſmall cornelian ſaucer.

Two antique Roman ear-rings, one with a pearl, the other of gold. M.

A box in compartments of old Japan.

A ſmall

A ſmall buſt in bronze of a Caligula, with ſilver eyes. This exquiſite piece is one of the fineſt things in the collection, and ſhews the great art of the ancients. It is evidently a portrait, carefully done, and ſeems to repreſent that emperor at the beginning of his madneſs. It was found with ſome other ſmall buſts at the very firſt diſcovery of Herculaneum, which happened by digging a well for the prince d'Elbœuf, who reſided many years afterwards at Florence, where it was ſold on his return to France, and, being purchaſed by ſir Horace Mann, was by him ſent to Mr. Walpole.

A broken patera engraved. M.

A ſacrificing inſtrument in the ſhape of a ſhell. M.

A Roman bulla of gold, very rare: bought at Rome of Ficaroni, who wrote his book of La Bolla d'oro from this.

A lady's head, miniature, ſet in gold: given to Mr. Walpole by Iſabella de Jonghe, counteſs of Denbigh.

A cryſtal ſceptre, ſet in gold enamelled, with pearls; from lady E. Germaine's collection, and given to Mr. Walpole by her niece lady Temple.

A cup and ſaucer of Seve china, blue ground with white heads and feſtoons.

A dreſſing-box and tray of the fineſt old ſilver japan.

Two caudle cups of Chelſea china, claret colour and gold.

A magnificent miſſal, with miniatures by Raphael and his ſcholars, ſet in gold enamelled, and adorned with rubies and turquoiſes; the ſides are of cornelian, engraved with religious ſubjects; the claſp, a large garnet. This precious prayer-book belonged to Claude queen of France, wife of Francis I. and ſeems to have belonged to the father of Thuanus; *vide vol.* 1. p. 142, *of the French edition.* It was purchaſed by Mr. Walpole from the collection of doctor Meade, 1755.

A ſilver Turkiſh ornament, taken by a Ruſſian officer in the laſt war; brought over by Charles lord Cathcart, and given by him to Margaret lady Brown, and by her to Mr. Walpole.

A round

A round ſnuff-box, enamelled with the ſtories of Joſeph and Potiphar's wife, Suſannah and the elders, Lot and his daughters, and a landſcape.

A gold ſnuff-box, enamelled: at top, a miniature of James I. and within, of queen Elizabeth; an onyx at bottom.

A ſmall ſnuff-box ſet in gold, with a fragment of a fine antique cameo in groteſque foliage on ſardonyx; from the Arundelian collection.

A needle-caſe, with monkeys, of old Japan.

Two boxes in compartments, ditto.

Two ſmall ewers of bronze. M.

A tea-kettle of Chineſe ſilver, richly chaſed.

An agate oval caſket.

Henry VIIIth's dagger, of Turkiſh work; the blade is of ſteel damaſked with gold, the caſe and handle of chalcedonyx, ſet with diamonds and many rubies. From the collection of lady Elizabeth Germaine. The ducheſs of Portland has ſuch another ſet with jacinths.

Antique figure of a muſe caſt in ſilver; ſitting: given to Mr. Walpole by lord Frederic Campbell, from the collection of his father John duke of Argyll.

Four ſmall Japan boxes.

A boy's head modelled in wax on copper, by Abraham Simon.

A ditto with a bulla, in Roman glaſs.

A large amethyſt, ſet coarſely in gold. It belonged to the ſecond biſhop of Landaff, and was given by doctor John Ewer biſhop of Landaff, in whoſe *time it was found, to doctor Frederic Keppel biſhop of Exeter, and by him to his wife's uncle Mr. Walpole.

One of the only ſeven mourning rings given at the burial of Charles I. It has the king's head in miniature; behind, a death's head between the

* Anno 1764.

letters C. R. The motto, *Prepared be to follow me.* A present to Mr. Walpole from lady Murray Elliot.

An urn, cameo on onyx, mourning ring for Henrietta Hobart countess of Suffolk.

An urn set with diamonds, mourning ring for Arthur Onslow, speaker of the house of commons.

A chimera, antique intaglia, a green stone in the ancient brass setting.

A small antique ring with the head of Cybele, all of one piece of gold.

A gold ring for a child, with a phallus; ditto.

A boy with his head in a scenic mask, on a red stone; antique, set in gold.

An Egyptian pebble representing exactly the portrait of a woman in profile, a rock behind her, sky before; set in gold.

Two pateras of bronze, engraved. M.

Ivory covers of a Roman pocket-book. M.

A fibula, a small votive foot, an agate ornament for a bridle, and some other small bronzes. M.

An Egyptian pebble, with a lusus naturæ that represents Voltaire in his night-gown and cap.

A small head in water-colours of Liotard, without his beard, by himself; a legacy from Mrs. Delany.

In the other glass case:

A leaf of a water-plant, gracefully tied up into the shape of a cup, with a saucer, of Chinese bronze.

Two vases of Chelsea porcelaine, claret colour, gold and white, with cartouches of historic figures.

Two long Japan boxes.

Two

Two Roman ſpears, a votive foot and toe.

A point cravat carved by Gibbons; a preſent from Mr. Groſvenoı Bedford.

An old enamelled watch, given by Mr. Ch. Churchill, junior.

A ſilver gilt reliquaire and chain; given to Mr. Walpole by George lord Edgcumbe.

An Etruſcan Mars; very barbarous.

A ſmall Egyptian figure ſitting, of baſaltes. M.

A naked man. M.

The ſeal of archbiſhop Dowdall, laſt popiſh primate of Ireland; in ſilver: from Mr. Briſtow's collection.

Two cups and a ſaucer of Milan ſtone.

Two caudle-cups of Chelſea porcelaine, blue with gold figures.

A Japan pomatum-pot.

A ſmall bloodſtone cup ſet in gold enamelled.

A ſmall cornelian box ſet in gold.

A triangular cornelian ſeal, with the heads of the two Fauſtinas and Lucilla, intaglias; by Chriſtian Reiſin.

A ſilver ſeal, extremely ancient, of Hugh Oneal, king of Ulſter; brought out of Ireland by Mr. William Briſtow.

A large ancient gold ring, with a caſtle on it, and within, *Un bon An*: found in the Thames.

A cornelian ſeal, with half figure of Omphale; antique intaglia. M.

Seal of Richard Clitherol, admiral for the weſt coaſts in the reign of Henry V.

Seal for indulgences of pope Eugenius.

Seal of the corporation of Pool.

Seal of the fraternity of ſaint Mary of Hitchin. Theſe four are of bronze and ancient: from Mr. Briſtow's collection.

A * ſpoon of Engliſh pebble, with gold handle of foliage.

A ſilver bottle for eſſences, that opens into ſeveral diviſions.

A ſmall buſt of Omphale in bronze.

A round flat box of ſilver filigraine.

A tooth-pick caſe of Egyptian pebble, and a ſmelling-bottle of agate.

A ſet of beads mounted in ſilver filigraine, taken in Spain in queen Anne's war by captain Galfridus Walpole, brother of ſir Robert.

A ſeal of the head of ſir Robert Walpole on white cornelian, by Natter; a preſent from Margaret lady Brown.

A ſilver popiſh medal mounted in filigraine.

A cup and ſaucer of Seve porcelaine, blue with white heads.

A dreſſing-box and tray of fine old gold Japan.

A tea-caniſter of ſtraw; on one ſide Meleager and Atalanta, on the other the arms of ſir Robert Walpole and Catherine Shorter.

A Japan dreſſing-box and tray of irregular ſhape.

Ditto, octagon, with tray and ſix round boxes within.

A Pollux, ſmall fine antique bronze. M.

A ſmall Terminus. M.

* There were a dozen of theſe ſpoons made by order of Catherine lady Walpole, as a preſent to queen Caroline, after whoſe death Mr. W. met with this and the handle of another in a toy-ſhop. The counteſs dowager, mother of R. earl of Burlington, was the firſt who countenanced the poliſhing of Engliſh pebbles, and gave a fine table of them, which is now at Chiſwick, to her ſon.

A round

A round white ſnuff-box; on the top, miniature of madame de Sevigné; at bottom, the cypher of Rabutin and Sevigné in marcaſites. This box, with the letter * in it from madame de Sevigné in the Elyſian fields to Mr. Walpole, was ſent to him by madame du Deffand.

A toothpick-caſe of gold, enamelled with cameos; a preſent from lady Diana Beauclerc.

A gold ſnuff-box, with the image in wax of mad. du Deffand's dog, Tonton, whom ſhe bequeathed with this ſnuff-box and her MSS. to Mr. Walpole.

A green and white ſnuff-box of Dreſden porcelaine ſet in gold; a preſent from Francis earl of Huntingdon.

A bloodſtone ſeal ſet in old enamel, given to Mr. Walpole by Mrs. Henrietta Conway, daughter of Francis lord Conway.

A ſmelling-bottle of purple glaſs with peacock's feathers in gold.

Ditto of Chineſe ſilver.

A ſmall amber crucifix.

* Letter written by madame Marie de Vichy, marquiſe du Deffand [the lady to whom Mr. W. afterwards dedicated his edition of the Memoires de Grammont] in the name of madame de Sevigné from the Elyſian fields to Mr. Walpole, after his return from Paris in 1766:

" Des champs Eliſées.

[Point de ſucceſſion de tems, point de date.]

"Je connois votre folle paſſion pour moi; votre enthouſiaſme pour mes lettres, votre veneration pour les lieux que j'ai habités: J'ai apris le culte que vous m'y * avez rendu: j'en ſuis ſi penetrée, que j'ai ſollicité & obtenu la permiſſion de mes Souverains de vous venir trouver pour ne vous quitter jamais. J'abandonne ſans regret ces lieux fortunés; je vous prefere à tous ſes habitans: jouiſſez du plaiſir de me voir; ne vous plaignez point que ce ne ſoit qu'en peinture; c'eſt la ſeule exiſtence que puiſſent avoir les ombres. J'ai eté maîtreſſe de choiſir l'age où je voulois reparoître; j'ai pris celuy de vingt cinq ans pour m'aſſurer d'être toujours pour Vous un objet agreable. Ne craignez aucun changement; c'eſt un ſingulier avantage des ombres; quoique legeres, elles ſont immuables. J'ai pris la plus petite figure qu'il m'a eté poſſible, pour n'être jamais ſeparée de Vous. Je veux vous accompagner par tout, ſur terre, ſur mer, à la ville, aux champs; mais ce que j'exige de vous, c'eſt de me mener inceſſamment en France, de me faire revoir ma patrie, la ville de Paris, et de choiſir pour votre habitation le fauxbourg St. Germain; c'etoit là qu'habitoient mes meilleures Amies, c'eſt le ſejour des votres; vous me ferez faire connoiſſance avec elles: je ſerai bien aiſe de juger ſi elles ſont dignes de vous, & d'être les Rivales de

RABUTIN DE SEVIGNE.".

* *He had dined at Livri.*

A ſmall

A ſmall bronze figure of a woman with a rudder and cornucopia.

Model of the Great Duke's diamond.

In the box of antique rings:

Tiberius, cameo on onyx, of the firſt Greek workmanſhip.

Cupid driving a car with two butterflies; intaglia on cornelian.

A man's head; alto relievo on onyx.

An Egyptian goddeſs's head on a green ſtone. M.

A cock and cornucopia; intaglia on cornelian.

A bacchante and goat; fine cameo on onyx: given to Mr. Walpole by the princeſs de Craon.

Germanicus; very fine intaglia on cornelian, with the workman's name Epitu, for Epitynchanes: from the collection of the marquis Riccardi at Florence *.

Head of Jupiter; ditto: from ditto.

A ſcenic maſk; cameo on onyx.

Caius, nephew of Auguſtus; ditto.

A lion; intaglia on ſardonyx.

A caprice, on white cornelian; intaglia. M.

Apollo; intaglia on cornelian: a preſent from ſir Horace Mann.

Iſis; Egyptian cameo on onyx. M.

A Cicada; fine intaglia on cornelian.

* In baron Stoſch's collection of Pierres Gravées which have the names of their artiſts, there is another Germanicus with the name of the ſame workman Epitynchanes. It is larger than Mr. Walpole's, and repreſents that prince younger; but it is imperfect, the lower part being broken off directly from the chin.

A Syrian king; ditto. M.

Fauſtina ſenior; ditto.

Chriſtian inſcription; *Vitas luxuriam, Homo bone:* cameo on onyx.

Matidia; intaglia in a green paſte: a moſt rare head. M.

The Horatii; intaglia on çornelian: given by ſir Robert Walpole to his ſon Horatio.

Mercury; intaglia in amethyſt: given to Mr. Walpole by general Conway.

Jupiter Serapis; altiſſimo relievo in bloodſtone.

A ram's head; intaglia on cornelian. [*End of the rings.*

Old Japan plate of different colours.

Popiſh beads, bought at the church of ſaint Anthony of Padua.

Turkiſh beads enamelled with blue and gold; probably for ornaments in a proceſſion: bought at the ſale of monſieur Julienne, at Paris.

A ſmall wooden croſs, curiouſly carved.

A moſt beautiful ſilver bell, made for a pope by Benvenuto Cellini. It is covered all over in the higheſt relievo with antique maſks, flies, graſshoppers, and other inſects; the virgin and boy-angels at top, a wreath of leaves at bottom. Nothing can exceed the taſte of the whole deſign, or the delicate and natural repreſentation of the inſects: the wonderful execution makes almoſt every thing credible that he ſays of himſelf in his Life. It came out of the collection of the marquis of Leonati at Parma, and was bought by the marquis of Rockingham, who exchanged it with Mr. Walpole for ſome very ſcarce Roman medals of great bronze, amongſt which was an unique medaliuncino of Alexander Severus with the amphitheatre, in the higheſt preſervation.

Two Corniſh diamonds, one incloſing green, the other yellow moſs.

A bronze altar-pot and a tripod. M.

A large Goa ſtone.

A ſilver box, almoſt in the ſhape of an egg, engraved.

A ſmall box of the gold and white Japan. In it are two dates found in a jar at Herculaneum; they are burnt to a coal, but the ſhapes and rivelled ſkins are entire.

A cornelian ſpoon that belonged to Coſſim Aly Caun.

An amber toothpick-caſe.

A tortoiſeſhell ſnuff-box, the top repreſents Flemiſh lace; given to Mr. Walpole by lady Mary Coke.

A round ſnuff-box, and an egg-ſhaped ditto.

Pictures and Bronzes in other parts of the Tribune.

Side oppoſite to the door:

A drawing by Mr. Bentley, repreſenting two lovers in a church looking at the tombs of Abelard and Eloiſa, from theſe lines of Pope,

If ever chance two wand'ring lovers brings
To Paraclete's white walls and ſilver ſprings, &c.

Chriſt and Mary Magdalen in the garden, in water-colours; by Catherine lady Walpole.

Two flower-pieces; by Baptiſte Monoyer.

Chriſt laid in the ſepulchre, after the fine picture of Parmegiano at Houghton; by Mr. Horace Walpole.

Two more flower-pieces; by Baptiſte Monoyer.

Madonna and child; by Salſa Ferrata, after Guido.

Correggio's Magdalen copied in crayons by Roſalba.

Temptation

Temptation of ſaint Antony; by Teniers.

Story of Celadon and Aſtrea, in water-colours; by W. Baur.

St. George, in altiſſimo relievo in ſilver.

Frances Howard, the famous counteſs of Eſſex and Somerſet; by Iſaac Oliver: from Mr. Weſt's collection.

Vandyck's head, by himſelf; a ſketch for the duke of Grafton's picture.

Soldiers at cards, a curious picture, being painted in the manner of Teniers, by Vandyck; from lord Oxford's collection.

The education of Cyrus, in water-colours, by Judith Boiſſiere, a French woman, in 1725: from Caſtiglione, in the collection at Houghton.

A wreath of flowers; octagon; by Phil. Laura: in the middle, head of Roſalba's Tiroleſe girl, by Carlevares, a female ſcholar of Roſalba.

Cornelius Polemberg, by himſelf, oval on copper; exquiſitely finiſhed like enamel, yet with great freedom.

His wife, by ditto; inferior in freedom and labour. Theſe two from ſir Robert Walpole's collection.

A beautiful bronze vaſe, taken from the antique by Fiamingo, who has added fine bas-reliefs of boys: from the Harleian collection.

A young gladiator in bronze. M.

A young Hercules, ditto, with the lion's ſkin on his arm; fine. M.

An antique ewer of bronze; a greyhound reaching to drink forms the handle: a preſent from Charles Churchill, eſq.

A very rare figure of Diana of Epheſus, in ſerpentine ſtone.

A green Egyptian figure, one of thoſe found in the pyramids.

Pictures and bronzes on the ſide where the altar is:

A man and woman ſitting: by Watteau; from ſir Robert Walpole's collection *.

* All the pictures that were not at Houghton were ſold after his death.

Thompſon, printſeller; by Riley.

An oval hunting-piece, by Wyck; from ſir Robert Walpole's collection.

Mary queen of Scots, whole length in water-colours; by Vertue, from the picture at Hatfield.

A merry-making, very neat; by a Swiſs lady.

A rural ball; ditto.

St. Sebaſtian; by Goltzius.

An old woman's head; by Gerard Dow.

Boys with vines on a monument; from ſir Robert Walpole's collection: by Philippo Laura.

Chriſt as a pilgrim, and ſaint Catherine, crowned by an angel: by Taddeo Zucchero.

A calm ſea with ſhips; by Samuel Scott.

The engagement between the Lion and Elizabeth in the year 1745; the young pretender was on board the latter: by ditto.

The Florentine boar in bronze.

A ſmall bronze vaſe, with a ſacrifice to Priapus.

A larger, ditto. Theſe two from Dr. Meade's collection.

A bronze bull.

An Egyptian hieroglyphic hand: bronze.

A ſphinx; ditto. M.

Pictures and bronzes on the ſide oppoſite to the altar:

A dog drinking; by Caſtiglione.

Two more flower-pieces; by Baptiſte Monoyer.

Two

Two larger; by young Baptiſte.

Charlotte de la Tremouille, grand-daughter of William the great prince of Orange, and wife of James Stanley earl of Derby, who was beheaded in the civil war: ſhe defended Latham-houſe for ſeveral weeks againſt the republicans.

The virgin and child, with other ſaints; a capital drawing by Parmegiano.

Ulyſſes diſcovering Achilles among the daughters of Lycomedes; by Wermer, in water-colours, after Nicolo Pouſſin. The architecture is moſt beautiful, and in the roof Pouſſin has judiciouſly introduced an ancient bas-relief with The judgment of Paris, as connected with the ſtory of Achilles.

Madame Suarez, a Florentine beauty; in crayons, by Roſalba.

Madame de Sevigné, when a young widow.

Madame de Grignan. Theſe two are ovals on copper, by Müntz.

A woman carrying a pig to be ſacrificed; bronze. M.

A lamp with a ſatyr's head; ditto: copied from the antique.

An antique lamp, of bronze, with a face.

Sketch of the head of Roger Palmer earl of Caſtlemaine, huſband of the ducheſs of Cleveland; by ſir Godfrey Kneller.

Chriſt depoſited in the ſepulchre: by Mola, after Raphael.

Chriſt praying in the garden; by Philippo Laura: from the collection of monſieur Julienne.

Margaret Cecil lady Brown, in crayons; by Roſalba.

Madame de la Fayette, on copper; by Müntz.

Lady Mary Coke *, in wax; by Goſſet.

Raphael's Jonas, in ivory.

* Lady Mary Campbell, fourth daughter of John duke of Argyll and Greenwich, widow of Edward lord Coke, only ſon of Thomas earl of Leiceſter. This was the lady to whom Mr. W. dedicated the Caſtle of Otranto.

A beau-

A beautiful lamp, in the ſhape of a foot, Cupid fallen aſleep over the flame; antique bronze with ſilver ornaments: it was found in the temple of Cupid, is publiſhed by Montfaucon, and was bought at the ſale of the Harleian collection.

Another bronze lamp.

Pictures and bronzes on the door-ſide:

A landſcape; by Müntz.

Two hermits; after Rubens.

Two flower-pieces; by young Baptiſte.

A Dutch ſurgeon dreſſing a boor's leg; from ſir Robert Walpole's collection.

The circumciſion; by Ludovico Caracci, on copper; a deſign for an altar-piece which he executed at Bologna.

A farm-yard; moſt natural.

Young Hercules with the ſerpents; by Annibal Caracci.

St. George; painted by Gioſeppe d'Arpino on lapis lazuli.

Sir Godfrey Kneller, when young; by himſelf: great ſpirit. Theſe four laſt from ſir Robert Walpole's collection.

A Roman emperor in bronze, as an idol, with thunderbolt and caduceus. M.

Two Roman lamps of bronze; one Chriſtian, of the latter empire.

Sir Peter Lely, in crayons; by himſelf.

Rubens, his wife and child, in water-colours, by B. Lens, from the original at Blenheim.

A battle, in black and gold, exquiſitely touched by Callot: bought at Mrs. Stanley's ſale.

The

The virgin and child in the clouds, the city of Bologna beneath; by Goupy, after Annibal Caracci.

A drunken boor; by Brauwer.

Head of an abbé; by Teniers: from the collection of monsieur Hareng.

Bust of an emperor, in black marble.

A bagpiper; bronze. M.

A sacrificing priest; ditto. M.

N. B. *All the bronzes, lamps, &c. stand on brackets under the pictures.*

IN THE PASSAGE,

OVER the entrance of which is an owl in cut paper, by Bermingham,

An Indian bottle and pipe, ornamented with gold and pearls; brought from Bengal by Henry Churchill, esq. in 1776.

A flower in paper mosaics, by Miss Jennings.

A head in profile of Robert Vere earl of Oxford and duke of Ireland, favourite of Richard II. from Mr. Scott's collection.

Mary duchess of Richmond, daughter of George Villiers, duke of Bucks; small whole length from Vandyck.

Head of Fiamingo the sculptor, holding an ivory group of boys.

Drawing of a concert, by captain Laroon.

View of the cathedral of Gloucester, by Samuel Lysons, esq. 1785.

View of Windsor-castle, by lady Diana Spencer, duchess of Bedford.

Print of monsieur le duc de Nivernois.

A scene in act 4th of the Mysterious Mother, by Westall.

THE SMALL CLOSET.

VENUS and Cupid in ivory, finely drawn and executed, but in the Flemish style; a present from Mr. Watson the surgeon.

An ivory comb, sent by pope Gregory to queen Bertha; from the Portland collection.

A view of the castle of Otranto as it really exists: a washed drawing; given by lady Craven.

A model of the druidical temple that was discovered in Jersey, in 1786, and was presented by the states of the island to their governor general Conway, and is now erected at his seat at Park-place in Berkshire.

A flower in paper mosaic, by Mrs. Delany; a legacy from her.

THE GREAT NORTH BEDCHAMBER

IS hung with crimson Norwich damask. The bed is of tapestry of Aubusson, festoons of flowers on a white ground, lined with crimson silk; plumes of ostrich feathers at the corners. Six elbow chairs of the same tapestry, with white and gold frames; and six ebony chairs. A carpet of the manufacture of Moorfields; a foot-carpet of needle-work; and a fire-screen of the tapestry of the Gobelins.

The chimney was designed by Mr. Walpole from the tomb of W. Dudley bishop of Durham, in Westminster-abbey, and is of Portland stone, gilt; with dogs of or moulu with arms and trophies: the chimney-back is ancient, and bears the arms of Henry VII. On the hearth, two old red china bottles.

Over the chimney, a large picture of Henry VIII. and his children; bought out of the collection of James West, esq. in 1773. *See a description of this curious piece in the Anecdotes of Painting.* On the chimney,

A bust of Francis II. king of France, husband of Mary queen of Scots.

A bronze bas-relief in profile of Anne of Bretagne, queen of Charles VIII.

and

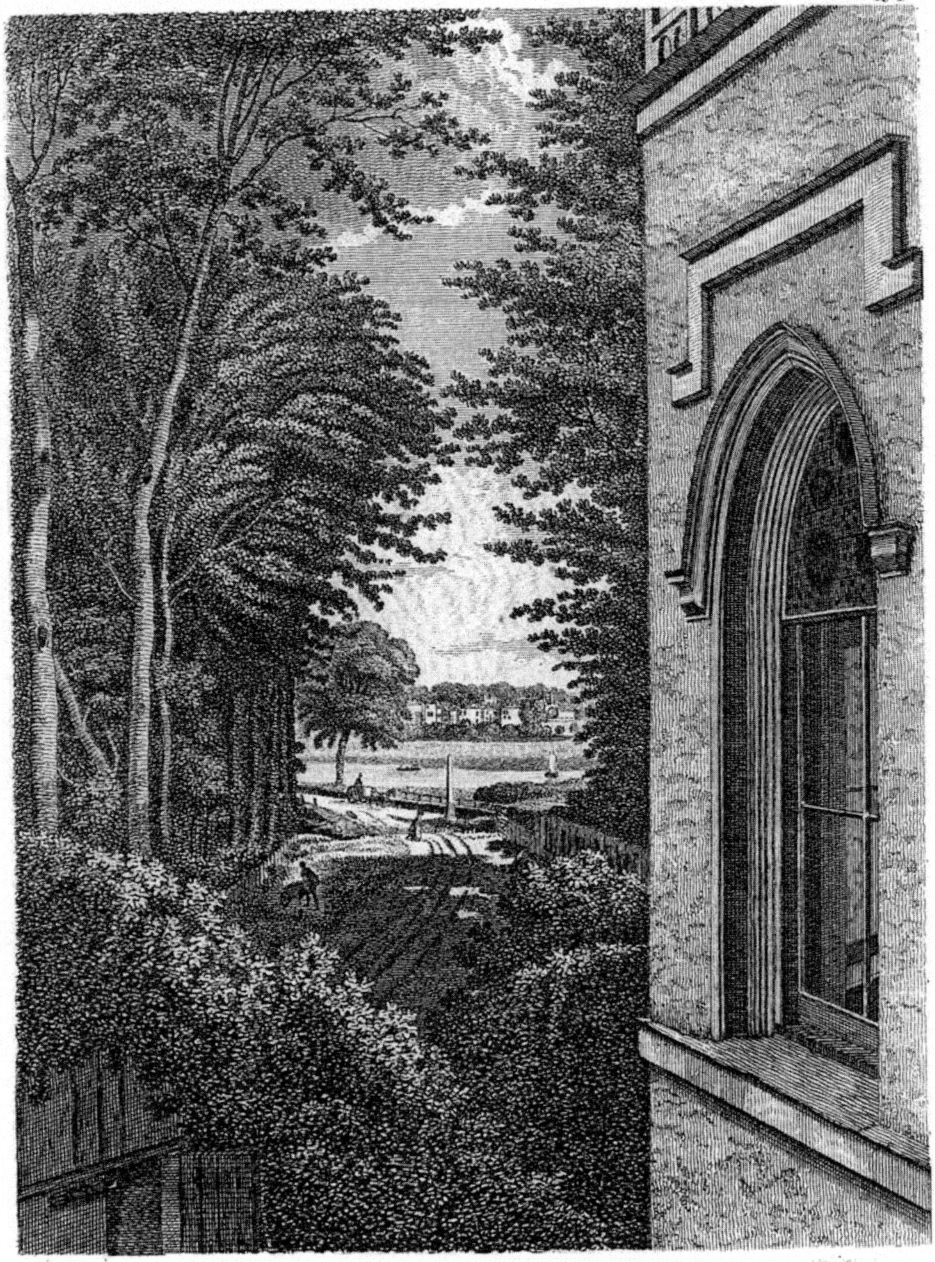

View from the great Bedchamber
AT STRAWBERRYHILL.

and of Louis XII. These two heads from the collection of the count de Caylus.

A nautilus mounted in silver gilt, with satyrs and the arms of Paston.

A crystal tankard and cover, mounted in silver gilt. These two pieces belonged to the last earl of Yarmouth.

Four old blue and white china bottles.

Two bas-reliefs of boys in wax on glass, designed and modelled by lady Diana Beauclerc, sister of George duke of Marlborough. On the back are written these lines:

Tho' taste and grace thro' all my limbs you see,
And nature breathes her soft simplicity,
Me nor Praxiteles nor Phidias form'd;
'Twas Beauclerc's art the sweet creation warm'd,
From Marlbro' sprung.—We in one heav'n-born race
Th' attemper'd rays of the same genius trace;
As big with meteors from one cloud depart
Majestic thunder and keen lightning's dart. H. W.

On one side of the chimney, a fine whole length, by Vandyck, of Margaret Smith, wife of Thomas Carye, groom of the bedchamber to Charles I. From the Wharton collection, afterwards in that of sir Robert Walpole.

On the other side, Philip Herbert earl of Pembroke and Montgomery, (with a view of old Wilton) whole length; by Mytens.

On one side of the bed, a whole length of Henry Vere earl of Oxford, in his robes. He was made knight of the bath at the creation of Henry prince of Wales, and died in Flanders in 1625.

On the other side, Robert Walpole, second earl of Orford; whole length, in robes of the bath; by Vanloo.

On the side opposite to the bed:

Frances, daughter of Richard Jennings, esq. [the mademoiselle Jennings of Grammont]

Grammont] first married to George Hamilton, and afterwards to Richard Talbot duke of Tyrconnel: copy by Milbourn from the original at lord Spencer's.

Two views of Venice; by Mariefki.

A fine landscape with cattle; by Gaspar Poussin.

The duchesse de la Valiere, mistress of Louis XIV. given by the duchess dowager of Portland.

Mademoiselle Hamilton, comtesse de Grammont; copy after Lely, by Eckardt.

Ninon L'Enclos, the only original picture of her; given by herself to the countess of Sandwich, daughter of Wilmot earl of Rochester, and by her grandson John earl of Sandwich to Mr. Walpole.

Richard I. prisoner to the archduke of Austria; highly finished by Mieris.

The presentation in the temple; its companion: by Rembrandt*.

Over the doors, which were designed by Mr. Chute, and have medallions of Louis XIV. and Charles V. in bronze,

Madame de Maintenon; and Hortense Mancini duchess of Mazarin: the latter a copy from Carlo Maratti, at the duke of St. Alban's.

A small japan cabinet; a dejeuné of Seve china, blue and white with coloured birds; and a blue and white old china jar.

On the window side:

A large looking-glass in a rich ebony frame; and two bronze arms with masks, for candles.

Over the glass, the original portrait of Catherine of Braganza, that was sent from Portugal previous to her marriage with Charles II. and from which Faithorne scraped his print: a present from Richard Bull, esq.

* These two pictures were bought of a very old gentlewoman, for whose grandfather they had been painted, and till then had never been taken out of their old black frames.

A table

A table of Saracen moſaic, ſent to Mr. Walpole from Rome by ſir William Hamilton, mounted on an ebony frame, with two ebony ſtands.

An ewer and two beakers, of Roman fayence ; a preſent to Mr. Walpole from miſs Speed, afterwards married to the comte de Virri, miniſter from Turin.

A ſmall table with a landſcape of Seve porcelaine, mounted in old japan ; a legacy to Mr. Walpole from Mary lady Hervey.

In the window, two china porcelaine ſtools.

Richard Wellborn, maſter of requeſts temp. Henry VIII. He was deſcended from a younger ſon of Simon de Montford earl of Leiceſter, on whoſe death, to ſecure himſelf, he changed his name to Wellborn : a preſent from the earl of Exeter.

Sir Nicholas Carew, knight of the garter and maſter of the horſe to Henry VIII. in whoſe reign he was beheaded : copied by Milbourn from the original by Holbein, at Beddington in Surrey.

Sir John Perrot, lord deputy of Ireland in the time of queen Elizabeth; in black and white chalk, by Chambars, from the original at ſir Herbert Perrot Packington's.

The original ſketch of the Beggar's Opera : Walker, as Macheath ; miſs Fenton, afterwards ducheſs of Bolton, as Polly ; Hippiſley, as Peach'em ; Hall, as Lockit : on one ſide in a box, ſir Thomas Robinſon, very tall and lean ; ſir Robert Fagg, a famous horſe-racer, fat, with ſhort grey hair ; by Hogarth. Bought at the ſale of John Rich, the well-known harlequin, and maſter of the theatres in Lincoln's-inn-fields and Covent-garden, for whom the picture was painted.

Van Helmont, the chymiſt ; copied by Müntz from a fine original by ſir Peter Lely, at the earl of Hertford's at Ragley.

Lady Henrietta Berkeley, ſiſter-in-law and miſtreſs of Ford lord Grey in the reign of Charles II. Bought at lady Suffolk's ſale.

Mary princeſs of Orange, daughter of king Charles I. given to Mr. Walpole by the prince of Monaco.

Rehearſal of an opera, with caricatures of the principal performers: Nicolini ſtands in front, Mrs. Toft is at the harpſichord, Margarita is entering in black *. Bought at the ſale of John duke of Argyll, who bought it at that of Charles Stanhope, eſq. By Sebaſtian Ricci: the landſcape in it by Marco Ricci.

Henry VII. a moſt capital portrait on board, and incomparable for the truth of nature, expreſſion and chiaro ſcuro. The character and thought in the countenance, and its exact conformity with the buſt by Torreggiani in the Star-chamber, make it unqueſtionably a portrait for which the king ſat; and yet the knowledge of light and ſhade, not poſſeſſed even by Holbein, makes it probable that this picture was retouched by Rubens, of whoſe colouring it is worthy and reſembles.

A table painted by lady Anne Fitzpatrick, daughter of the earl of Oſſory.

In the bow windows are ten coats of arms in painted glaſs, by Peckitt of York, with the principal matches of the family of Walpole.

The ceiling was copied from one at the Vine in Hampſhire.

Curioſities in the glaſs cloſet in the great bedchamber:

A ſalver of Raphael fayence, ſtory of The prodigal ſon.

A large diſh, ditto, ſtory of Abſalom.

One ditto, ſmaller, ſtory of Jael and Siſera.

A large plate, ditto, Feaſt of the gods.

One ſmaller, Chriſt walking on the water.

One ditto, cupids in relievo, ribbed border.

Ditto, Apollo and Marſyas, ſcolloped border.

Two ſmall ditto, with landſcapes and buildings.

* The gentleman in blue, with a patch on one eye, ſitting by the Margarita, is ſir Robert Rich, father of Elizabeth lady Lyttelton. See curious accounts of Mrs. Toft and the Margarita in the 5th vol. of ſir John Hawkins's Hiſtory of Muſic.

Two ditto, twelve ſquare, very coarſe.

Two ten ſquare diſhes of the old dragon china.

A fine ſilver trunk to hold perfumes, with bas-reliefs, the top from Raphael's Judgment of Paris ; the work of Benvenuto Cellini. Bought out of the Great Duke's wardrobe ; a preſent from ſir Horace Mann.

A Chineſe ſteelyard.

An amber ſtanding cup and cover, from Mrs. Kennon's collection.

A bottle of purple glaſs *. This and all the following articles marked with an aſteriſm, were bought at the ſale of count Caylus at Paris.

Seven boxes of the old gold and white japan, with ſmaller boxes of the ſame within.

A ſilver gilt plate in relievo, the meeting of Charles V. and Francis I. a preſent from ſir William Hamilton.

A pair of gloves worn by king James the firſt: bought out of Thoreſby's muſeum.

The wedding gloves of Mrs. Hampden, wife of the celebrated John Hampden.

An agate puncheon with the arms of Mr. Gray the poet, and a Goa ſtone ; given to Mr. Walpole by doctor Browne and Mr. W. Maſon, Mr. Gray's executors.

A carved bottle for perfumes, mounted in ſilver ; Indian.

A bronze perfume pot.

A clouded ewer of poliſhed earth.*

An ewer of Villeroy ware.

Three packs of Florentine cards, for playing at Minchiati and Tarocco.

Rubens's child, in biſcuit china of Nancy.

Three French ſnuff-boxes mounted in gold.

Small ivory box, containing a ſuite of prints repreſenting medals on the victories in the war at the end of the reign of George II.

A ſnuff-box with views of Spa; given by miſs Churchill.

Two enamel plates, preſents from Caroline lady Greenwich.

A ſilver gilt apoſtle-ſpoon. Addiſon, in the Drummer, mentions apoſtle-ſpoons; and ſo do Beaumont and Fletcher in one of their plays. It was an ancient faſhion to have a little figure at the end of a ſpoon's handle, as this has. It was a preſent from the reverend Mr. W. Cole.

Three ditto, ungilt.

An antique bronze of a man, naked, the head of ſir Robert Walpole added by Nattier.

Small octagon diſh of old china with figures.

Nineteen draftſmen of box, with heads of German princes and princeſſes; a preſent from Charles duke of Richmond.

Fourteen more, bought at Mr. Bateman's ſale.

Two vaſes of blue china mounted in or moulu.

A blue and white plate with the brown edge, old china.

A ſmaller with dragons, without the border.

Two octagons of blue and white with figures, pierced.

Two hexagon ſaucers, ditto, with feet.

A box with ancient round trenchers, with ſcriptural mottos; a preſent from the reverend Mr. W. Cole.

A German pitcher and cover, with bas-reliefs of figures dancing.*

Two plates of Chantilly china, of different ſizes.

A tea-pot of the old red japan ware.

Another red and black, of china.

A Turkiſh

A Turkiſh mug, with characters.*

An earthen pot, Indian.*

A blue and white earthen barrel, with handles.*

A drinking-veſſel of black earth, with ditto.*

A ſaltcellar of old fayence ſupported by dolphins.

Two blue and white diſhes and ſeven plates of old china; a legacy from Mrs. Henrietta Conway, ſiſter of Francis earl of Hertford.

Two old blue and white water-plates.

A copper diſh with a foot, enamelled with the ſtory of Abraham and Melchizedec; a preſent from George William Hervey earl of Briſtol.

A baſket of Seve china, blue, gold and white.

A Staffordſhire Etruſcan vaſe.

A blue vaſe of antique Roman glaſs with a boy's head.*

Four water-plates of old coloured china.

An urn and cover of Volterra alabaſter.

Two ewers of ancient glaſs.*

A blue and white ſquare pot for flowers, of old china.

A ſpeculum of kennel-coal, in a leathern caſe. It is curious for having been uſed to deceive the mob by Dr. Dee, the conjurer, in the reign of queen Elizabeth. It was in the collection of the Mordaunts earls of Peterborough, in whoſe catalogue it is called *the black ſtone into which Dr. Dee uſed to call his ſpirits.* From the Mordaunts it paſſed to lady Elizabeth Germaine, and from her to John laſt duke of Argyll, whoſe ſon, lord Frederic Campbell, gave it to Mr. Walpole.

A ſmall buſt in terra-cotta of Nicolo Pouſſin's wife, beautifully ſimple and natural, by Fiamingo, amicitiæ cauſâ; from monſ. Mariette's collection.

Two

Two ſquare flower-tubs of Wedgwood's ware, painted with antique cameos and maſks in blue, from deſigns of lady Diana Beauclerc.

The ſpurs worn by king William at the battle of the Boyne, preſerved in an Iriſh family, and given to the late earl of Harcourt when lord lieutenant, and by the preſent earl to Mr. W. in a red leather box lined with green velvet.

A tortoiſeſhell caſe ſtudded with ſilver, in which Van Tromp uſed to carry his pipes to ſea: a preſent from Mr. Hamilton.

Two ivory billiard-ſticks, engraved; they belonged to H. Herbert earl of Pembroke, and have his creſt a wyvern holding a bloody hand, and the bear and ragged ſtaff for his third wife, the famous Mary, ſiſter of ſir Philip Sidney; and an ancient ivory buſk, engraved with French devices and mottoes: all three from the collection of Mr. Goſtling at Canterbury.

Twelve ſilver deſſert-plates, engraved with the hiſtory of the prodigal ſon. They belonged to lord chancellor Clarendon, and deſcended to his great grand-daughter the celebrated ducheſs of Queenſberry, and were purchaſed at the duke's auction.

A ſmall tray of red japan.

A ſnuff-box beautifully painted in brown and white with figures from Etruſcan vaſes, beſpoken at Naples, and given by ſir William Hamilton.

An ancient German wooden ſpoon, curiouſly carved with religious figures and mottoes.

A vaſe of rock cryſtal, carved with battles, unfiniſhed, having been cracked in the workmanſhip, with a ſilver gilt foot; bought out of the Great Duke's wardrobe by ſir Horace Mann, and ſent to Mr. W.

An ebony cabinet, ornamented with or moulu, lapis lazuli, agates, pieces of ancient enamel, bas-reliefs of Wedgwood, and nine capital drawings of a gipſy girl and beautiful children by lady Diana Beauclerc, with other drawings by her; and with ſtrawberries and Mr. Walpole's arms and creſt. The deſign of the cabinet by Mr. E. Edwards, in 1783.

A ſnuff-

A ſnuff-box of red and white plaiſter, from the Piſcine mirabili at Rome; a preſent from miſs Campbell.

A ſnuff-box with moſaic pigeons, from the antique; a preſent from her royal highneſs the ducheſs of Glouceſter.

A large black ſtone baſon, made from the quarry with which the duke of Argyll's houſe at Inverary is built, and which is ſoft when firſt cut; given by Mr. Pinkerton.

In the cloſet-window is a head of queen Elizabeth in painted glaſs, and another pane with men playing at cards, very old.

On the BACK STAIRS.

Lady Catherine Fitzalan marchioneſs of Dorſet, daughter of William earl of Arundel, and firſt wife of Henry Grey, afterwards duke of Suffolk, from whom ſhe was divorced to make room for his marriage with lady Frances Brandon, daughter of Mary queen of France and Charles duke of Suffolk.

A large piece of ſtill life, by Adrian Van Utrecht.

The BEAUCLERC CLOSET

IS a hexagon, built in 1776, and deſigned by Mr. Eſſex, architect, of Cambridge, who drew the ceiling, door, window, and ſurbaſe. In the window is a lion and two fleurs de lys, royally crowned, ancient, but repaired and ornamented by Price; and, being bearings in the royal arms, ſerve for Beauclerc. The cloſet is hung with Indian blue damaſk, and was built on purpoſe to receive ſeven incomparable drawings of lady Diana Beauclerc for Mr. Walpole's tragedy of The Myſterious Mother. The beauty and grace of the figures and of the children are inimitable; the expreſſion of the paſſions moſt maſterly, particularly in the devotion of the counteſs with the porter, of Benedict in the ſcene with Martin, and the tenderneſs, deſpair, and reſolution of the counteſs in the laſt ſcene; in which is a new ſtroke of double paſſion in Edmund, whoſe right hand is clenched and ready to ſtrike with anger, the left hand relents. In the ſcene of the children, ſome are evidently vulgar, the others children of rank; and the firſt child, that pretends to look down and does leer upwards, is charming. Only two ſcenes are repreſented in all the ſeven, and yet all are varied; and the ground in the firſt, by a very uncommon effect, evidently deſcends and riſes again. Theſe ſublime drawings, the firſt hiſtories ſhe ever attempted, were all conceived and executed in a fortnight. Other pictures in this cloſet are,

Lady Diana Beauclerc, by Powel, after ſir J. Reynolds.

Charles Lenox third duke of Richmond, profile, by Milbourn after Romney.

Count Schouallow, favourite of the czarina Elizabeth, whoſe image he holds. This worthy man, who enjoyed abſolute power for twelve years, never did an injury or made an enemy. Painted at Paris in 1775.

Two young women and a boy, a drawing in a round, by lady Diana Beauclerc.

Four fronts of a gothic houſe, deſigned by Mr. John Chute for Mr. Andrews, and built at Spinehill near Donnington-caſtle, Berkſhire.

Two capital drawings by Paulo Panini, bought at Mariette's ſale.

A view of the fictitious monument deſigned and erected by general H. S. Conway, near the Thames, at his ſeat at Park-place near Henley: and

A view of the leſſer arch, deſigned and erected by the ſame, at ditto; with a ſmall portrait of the general himſelf. Theſe two by Paul Sandby, in 1781.

All theſe pictures have black and gold frames.

Two arms for candles, of or moulu, in the form of lilies, from Paris.

Two black and gold triangular ſtands.

A tea-ſervice of old blue and white porcelaine.

A tea-cheſt of Clay's ware, painted with looſe feathers.

A head of Auguſtus, from an antique cameo belonging to ſir William Hamilton, modelled in wax by Mrs. Damer, daughter of general Conway, in 1777.

A head of Voltaire, ditto, its companion.

I

A writing-

A writing-table of Clay's ware, highly varnifhed: it is black, with blue and white ornaments in a gothic pattern, defigned by Paul Sandby. In one of the drawers the play of The Myfterious Mother, to explain the drawings, bound in blue leather and gilt.

Four blue damafk ftools with black and gold frames.

The book of Pfalms, with 21 inimitable illuminations by don Julio Clovio, fcholar of Julio Romano. If any thing can excel the figures, it is the execution of the borders, which are of the pureft antique tafte, and unrivalled for the luftre and harmony of the colours, as well as for the prefervation, which is allowed to be more perfect than any of the few works of this extraordinary mafter. It was painted, as is faid on one of the illuminations, Principi Andegavenfi, 1537; was afterwards in the Arundelian collection; on the difperfion of which it was purchafed by the earl of Oxford in 1720, who bequeathed it to his daughter the duchefs of Portland, at whofe fale Mr. Walpole bought it in 1786.

The head of Jupiter Serapis, in bafaltes. The divine majefty and beauty of this precious fragment prove the great ideas and confummate tafte of the ancient fculptors. This buft was purchafed, with the celebrated vafe, from the Barberini collection at Rome, by fir William Hamilton; and was fold with the vafe to the duchefs of Portland, and on her grace's death was bought by Mr. Walpole.

A locket with hair of Mary Tudor, queen of France; whofe tomb was opened in 1784; a prefent from mifs Fauquier.

A very fmall cryftal watch; a prefent from general Fitzwilliam.

General Moncke, by Cooper.

The ROUND BEDCHAMBER, two Pair of Stairs.

THE infide of a church, a very good Flemifh picture on board; a legacy to Mr. Walpole from doctor Meyrick at Ifleworth.

Henrietta Hobart countefs of Suffolk, fitting; a view of her houfe at Marble-

Marble-hill, Twickenham: by Jervas. It was Mr. Pope's: lady Suffolk bought it at Mrs. Martha Blount's ſale, and gave it to Mr. Walpole.

Ogleby, the poet, in his ſhirt; fine, by Fuller: from ſir R. Walpole's collection.

Tillemans, the painter.

Mrs. Barry, the celebrated actreſs; profile, by ſir Godfrey Kneller. Sketch for the head of Britannia in the great equeſtrian picture of king William at Hampton-court.

Henrietta ducheſs of Orleans, as Pallas; bought at lady Suffolk's ſale.

The emperor Maximilian; a curious head.

Robert Dudley earl of Leiceſter.

Two half lengths of ladies, by ſir Peter Lely.

Chriſtian Reiſin, ſeal-engraver, in an oval; freely painted by Dahl.

Enoch Zeeman, the painter, in his original preſbyterian habit, and his daughter as a boy by him: well painted by himſelf.

Pearce, ſen. ſtatuary, by Fuller; from Vertue's collection.

Portrait of Oliver Cromwell's mother, copied from the original at Hinchinbrook; given by lord Sandwich.

Mrs. Catherine Clive, the actreſs, with a muſic-book; painted by Daviſon: a preſent from her brother Mr. James Raftor.

THE GREAT CLOYSTER.

AT each end, a blue and white china flower-pot; and in the middle, a fine antique marble vaſe, on a pedeſtal with a Greek inſcription; bought at the ſale of Chaſe Price, eſq. in 1778.

Eight very ancient Welch chairs, turned, and four ſtands; bought at the ſale of Mr. Richard Bateman of Old Windſor.

The

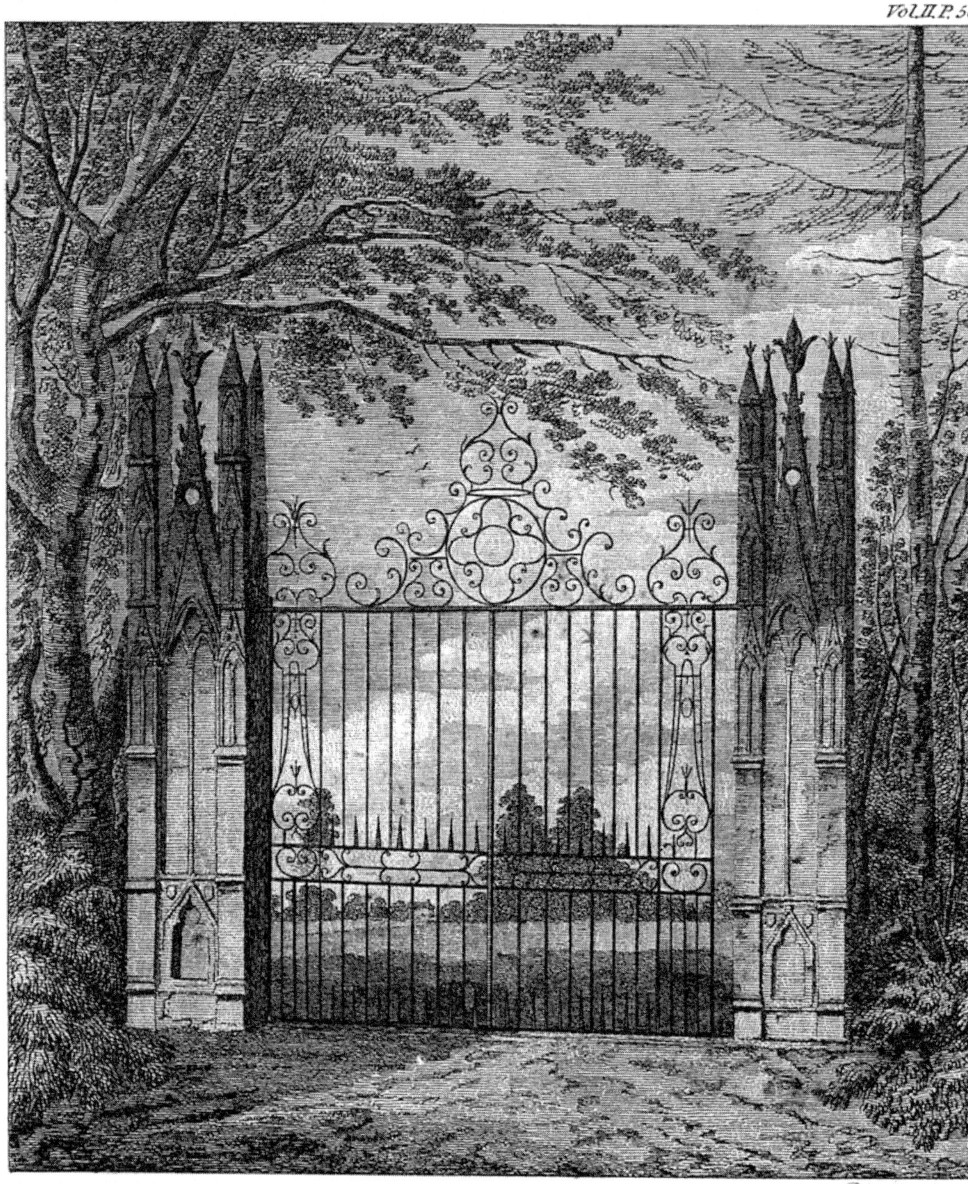

J. Morris sc.

GARDEN GATE.

The piers of the garden-gates are of artificial ſtone, and taken from the tomb of William de Luda biſhop of Ely, in that cathedral.

Before the chapel, ſtand on pedeſtals four rare Indian flower-tubs, bought at Mr. Bateman's.

THE CHAPEL,

IN the ſouth-weſt corner of the wood, is built of brick, with a beautiful front of Portland ſtone, executed by Mr. Gayfere of Weſtminſter, and taken from the tomb of Edmund Audley biſhop of Saliſbury, in that cathedral. In the anti-chapel is an oaken Gothic bench, deſigned by Mr. Bentley; over it, a head of ſaint John Baptiſt, alto-relievo, in marble, on a pedeſtal of the ſame in a fine taſte, the work of Donatello, and a preſent from ſir Horace Mann. On the oppoſite ſide, a crucifix of bronze; and beneath it, on an angular pedeſtal of fayence on which is a buſt of an angel, ſtands an encenſoir of bronze. By the door is a holy-water-pot of earthen-ware, given by Mr. G. A. Selwyn.

Four pannels that came out of the abbey of St. Edmundſbury, and were doors to an altar-piece, and were ſince in the poſſeſſion of Peter Leneve, Norroy, and after him of Mr. Martin and Mr. Ives, antiquaries; on whoſe death Mr. W. bought and had them ſawed into four pictures. On the outſide pannels are Henry Beaufort cardinal of Wincheſter, and John Kemp archbiſhop of Canterbury. On one of the inſides is Humphrey duke of Glouceſter praying, and behind him a ſaint holding the duke's cap of eſtate in one hand, and a golden chalice in the other. On the other is a perſon in the act of adoration in a ſtable, whence it is probable that the virgin and child were repreſented on the middle piece which is wanting. This perſon ſeems to be Joſeph, but may be the donor of the altar-piece, as over him is a ſhield of arms of Tate, impaling Boleyn or Sanders, for the colour of the chevron is turned black. Theſe perhaps might be attached to the houſe of Lancaſter, who were great benefactors to the abbey, and two princes of which family, afterwards ſo memorable for their enmity, are here repreſented. The three portraits agree remarkably with thoſe of the ſame perſons in the marriage of Henry VI. in the library, eſpecially the archbiſhop and the duke, who has the ſame bald head and furred mantle. The two prelates are hard and dry, but the duke and Joſeph are painted in

 a ſtyle

a ſtyle very ſuperior to that age, and the folds of their garments looſe and large, not unworthy of the Bologneſe ſchool.

In the window are the original portraits * of Henry III. and his queen in painted glaſs, with other ſaints and coats of arms. Fronting the door ſtands a magnificent ſhrine † of moſaic, three ſtories high; and beneath it, a crucifix ‡ inlaid with mother of pearl, bought at the ſale of the honourable Richard Bateman in 1774. On one ſide of the ſhrine, in a receſs, ſtands on a conſole a figure of an ancient king of France, in fayence; on the other ſide, the virgin Mary, of bronze. The roof was deſigned by Mr. Chute. On a tablet over the door is the following inſcription:

The ſhrine in front was brought in the year 1768 *from the church of Santa Maria maggiore in Rome, when the new pavement was laid there. This ſhrine was erected in the year* 1256 *over the bodies of the holy martyrs Simplicius, Fauſtina, and Beatrix, by John James Capoccio and Vinia his wife; and was the work of Peter Cavalini, who made the tomb of Edward the Confeſſor in Weſtminſter-abbey.* See The Anecdotes of Painting, p. 24.

The window was brought from the church of Bexhill in Suſſex. The two principal figures are king Henry III. and Eleanor of Provence his queen, the only portraits of them extant. King Henry died in 1272, *and we know of no painted glaſs more ancient than the reign of his father king John. Theſe portraits have been engraved for the frontiſpiece to The Anecdotes of Painting.*

This chapel was erected by Horace Walpole in the year 1771. *The façade was copied from a chapel-tomb in the cathedral of Saliſbury.*

At the end of the winding walk is a large ſeat in the form of a ſhell, carved in oak, from a deſign by Mr. Bentley.

* Theſe were a preſent from the earl of Aſhburnham.

† It was repaired, and parts ſupplied, by Richter, who made the chimney-piece in the round room; but he could not ſupply the golden glaſs in the original, the art of which is loſt.

‡ It ſtands on an angel and ſhield, which came out of Weſtminſter-abbey.

The

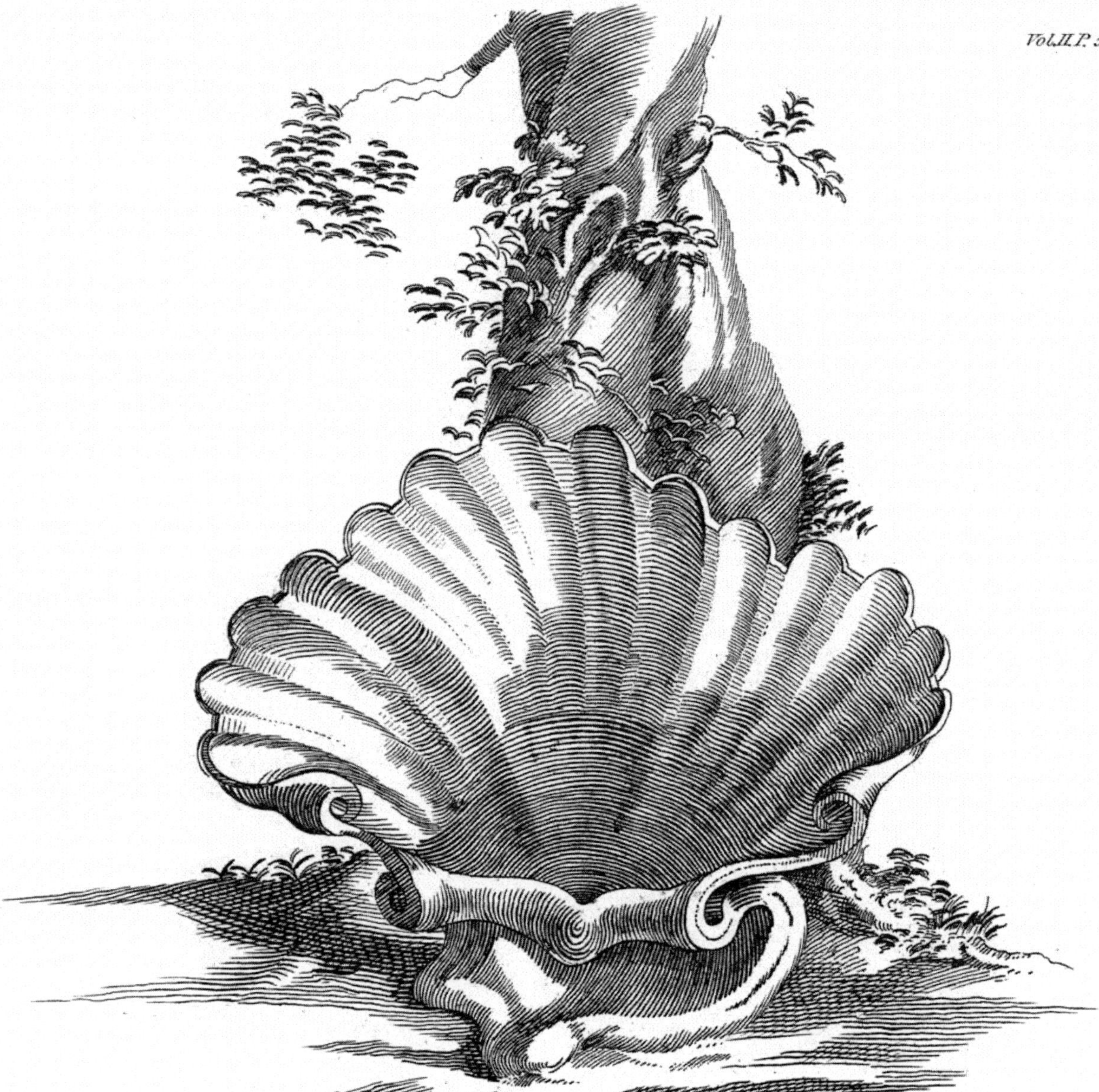

THE SHELL BENCH

J. Morris sc.

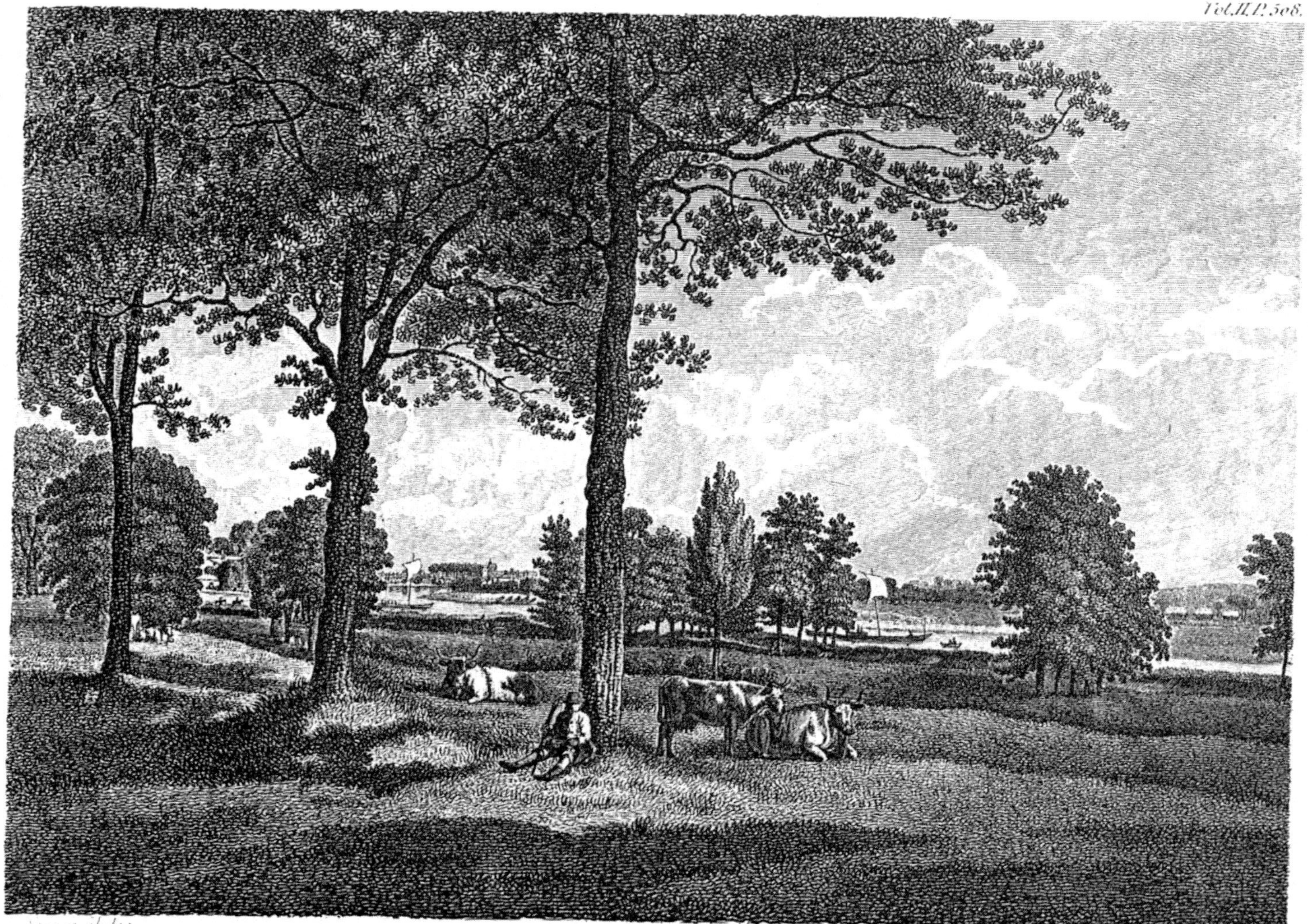

[illegible] delt. Godfrey Sc.

View from the Terrace at Strawberryhill.

The Cottage in the Flower-Garden.

The TEA-ROOM

IS hung with green paper and prints. Over the chimney, Mary Lepelle lady Hervey, by Ramſay, in a frame carved by Gibbons: from Mr. Bateman's. Two ſconces of Chantilly china; a ſceau for liquors, of Seve; two chocolate-cups, ditto; a handle-cup and ſaucer; a caudle-cup and deep ſaucer; all with coloured flowers. A rice-cup on feet; a ſaltcellar of old fayence; and four biſcuit figures. On the hearth, a large green vaſe of German ware, with a ſpread eagle, and lizards for handles. From Mr. Bateman's.

On a ſhelf and brackets, two pots-pourris of Nankin china; two pierced blue and white baſons of old Delft; and two ſceaus of coloured Seve; a blue and white vaſe and cover; and two old fayence bottles.

On the tea-table, a white tea-pot with gold edge, of Seve; four handle-cups and ſaucers, a ſugar-diſh, milk-pot, baſon, and plate, of the ſame; a tea-pot of crackled china with blue and brown flowers; an octagon green baſon with coloured flowers; a ditto, white, with ditto; a green leaf of Staffordſhire-ware; two blue and white handle-cups of Seve; one ditto larger, in ſhape of a pail; two ditto with coloured flowers and blue rims; one ditto with dark blue and gold edges and coloured flowers; and one ditto with blue and gold moſaic on white.

The LITTLE LIBRARY

IS painted green and white. Over the chimney, an original half-length of Milton, æt. 45, in black, a ring tied to one of his button-holes. In the key-ſtone of the chimney, an antique bas-relief with the ſtory of Mars and Venus. On the mantle-piece, ſeveral antique ſepulchral earthen lamps. On the hearth, a flower-pot of fine blue earth.

Four ancient Welch chairs: from Mr. Bateman's.

Over the door, an antique painting in freſco. *Vide Middleton's Germana, &c.*

A bronze tripod for burning incenſe. M.

A marble canopus.

Two ditto, ſmaller; bought at Mr. Bateman's.

Over the book-caſes, a ſmall marble buſt of lord chancellor Clarendon.

Several ſmall Etruſcan and black Staffordſhire vaſes.

Two yellow beakers, with flowers, of Staffordſhire ware.

Two red china ditto.

Two flower-pots of crackled china.

A blue china bottle.

A bronze inkſtand, in good taſte; from count Caylus's collection.

In this library are ſeveral volumes of MSS.

IN THE GARDEN,

AN extraordinary large brainſtone: a preſent from Mr. Groſvenor Bedford.

Bernini's Apollo and Daphne, in bronze.

A large antique ſarcophagus in marble, with bas-reliefs; from the collection of Bryan Fairfax, eſq.

Two oſſuaria.

The ſleeping Morpheus in plaiſter.

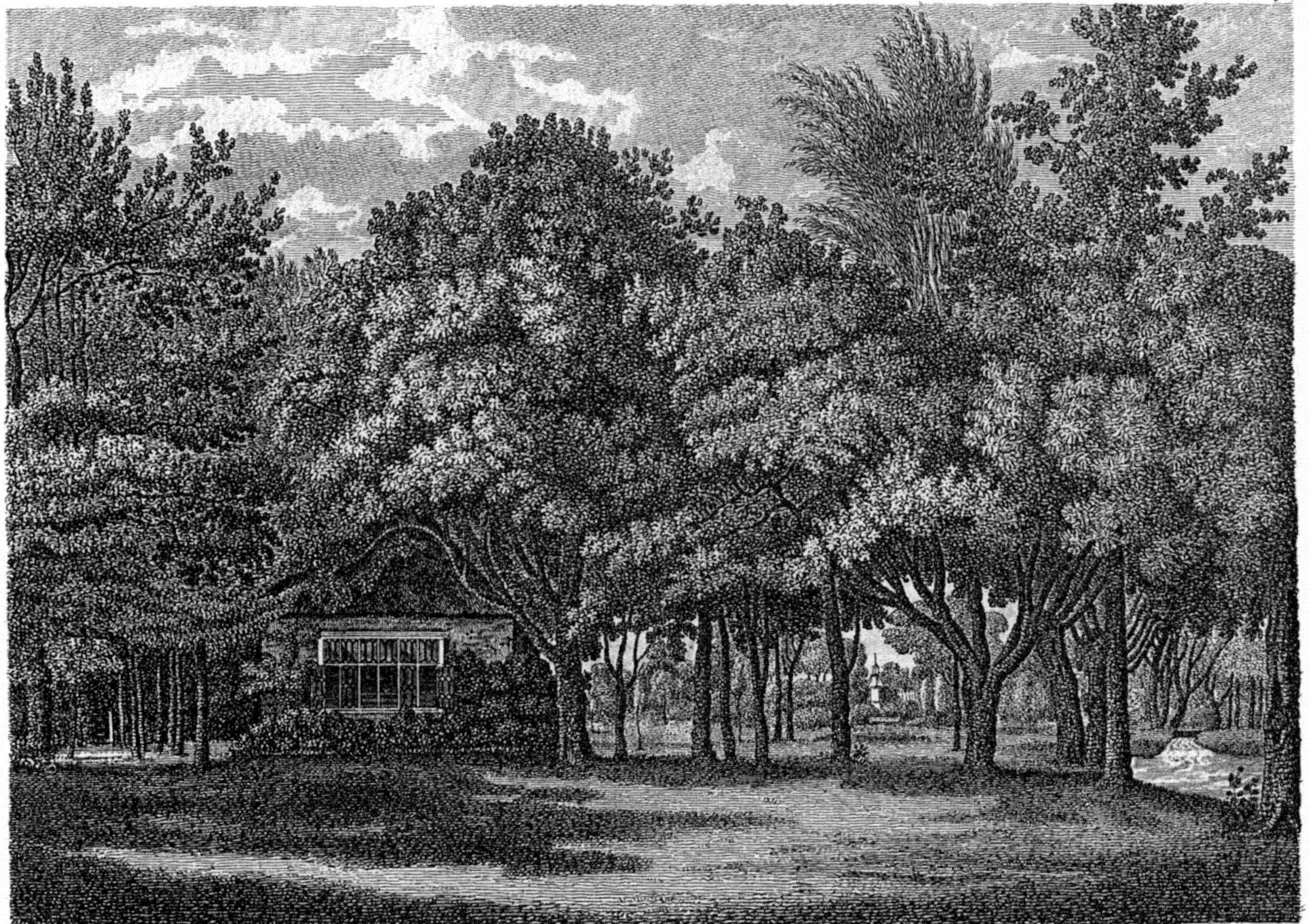

East View of the Cottage-garden at Strawberryhill.

ADDITIONS.

A Two-leaved ſcreen, painted on Mancheſter velvet, with the heads of a Satyr and Bacchante, by lady Diana Beauclerc, in 1788.

Twelve earthen plates, painted at Delft, with the ſigns of the zodiac, by ſir James Thornhill: bought at Mrs. Hogarth's ſale.

The death of cardinal Wolſey, copied by miſs Agnes Berry in water-colours, of the ſame ſize, and with all the ſtrength of the original in oil by Mr. William Lock—a ſublime compoſition, in which the expreſſions are worthy of the greateſt maſters, as the colouring and chiaro-ſcuro are equal to Rubens.

Proceſſion in the Caſtle of Otranto, in water-colours, by J. Carter.

A drawing, whole length, of Mrs. Damer, in the attitude of having juſt carved her young Paris; by Richard Coſway.

A ſmall head of Harris the actor, in the character of cardinal Wolſey, in oil. There is an unique print of it in the Pepyſian library at Cambridge.

A fox and partridge: and a water-dog and duck. Both by Oudry.

Frances Stuart, ducheſs of Richmond; oval head. *Vide Grammont.*

An emblematic braſs diſh, by Francis Briot.

A Venetian morion: and, a curious round helmet; engraved in captain Groſe's Armoury. Both bought at Mr. Rawle's ſale.

Johanna lady Abergavenny: *vide Royal and Noble Authors:* a preſent from miſs Beauclerc, the maid of honour.

An iron back of a grate, with general Fairfax on horſeback, dated 1649; found in the old kitchen at Strawberry-hill.

Lady Elizabeth Butler, counteſs of Cheſterfield; half length, by ſir Peter Lely: brought from her houſe at Breadby. *Vide Grammont.*

An

An ancient knife, with a curious handle of gold; a preſent from miſs Mary Carter.

The original portrait of Samuel Cooper, the miniature painter, from the royal collection; bought at Mr. Dalton's ſale.

Head of a gentleman, by Roſalba; ditto.

Prince Arthur, prince Henry, and princeſs Margaret, children of Henry the ſeventh, by Mabuſe; from Coſway's collection.

A rabbit, by Adrian Vandevelde; from ditto.

Thomas Wriotheſley earl of Southampton, lord treaſurer, by Samuel Cooper; from the collection of Mr. Browne, of Shipton-Mallet.

Two very large blue jars; from Mrs. French's collection.

An ewer of ancient fayence; ditto.

A ſmall vaſe of porphyry; from lord James Manners's collection.

A ſmall hamper of ſilver wire, containing a Goa ſtone; ditto.

A Scottiſh mull, made of a large ram's horn, and mounted in ſilver; a preſent from ſir James Colquhoun.

STRAW-

Vol.II.Pl.I.P.512.

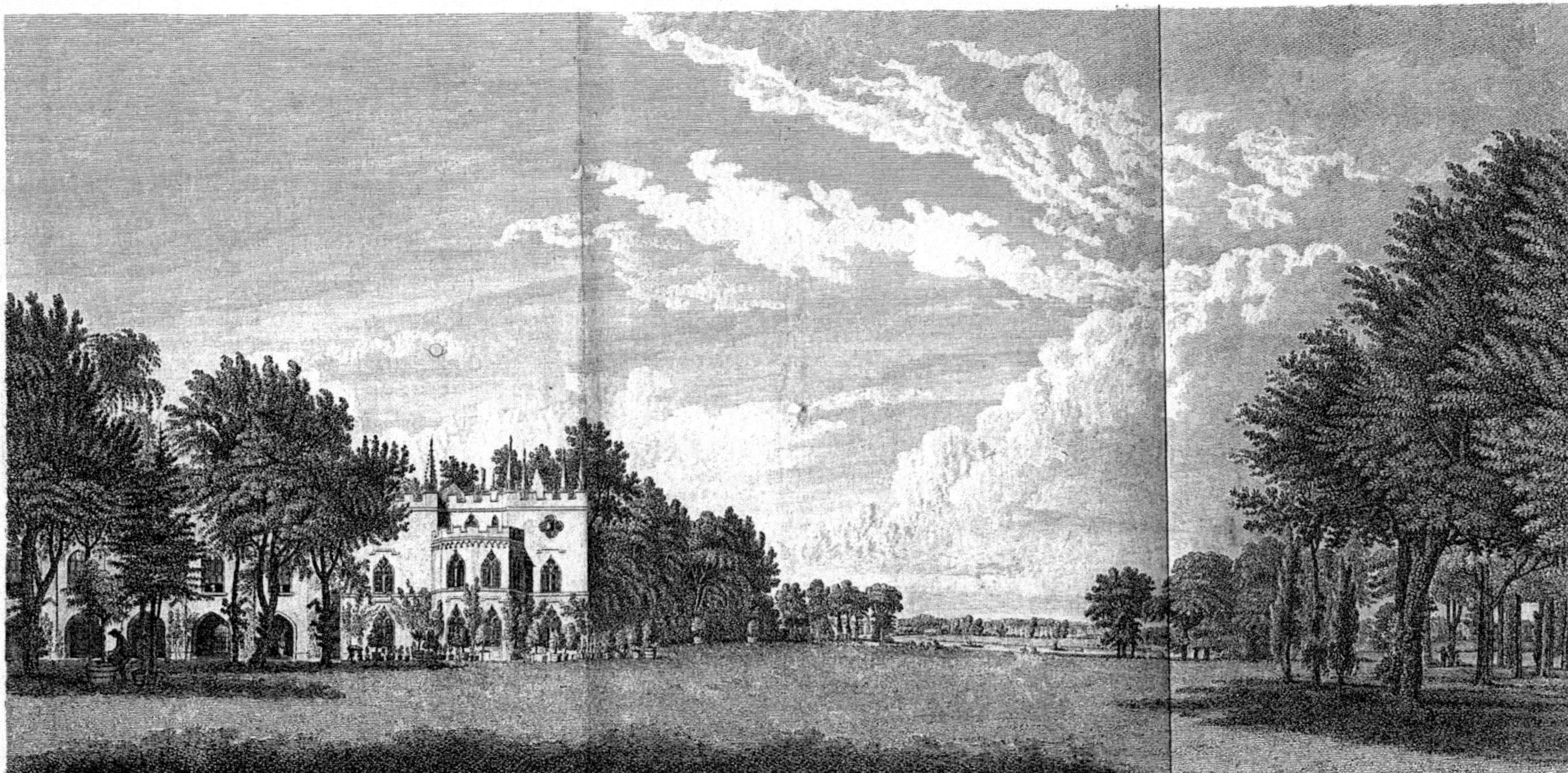

SOUTH FRONT OF STRAWBERRY HILL.

Vol. II. Pl. II. P. 312.

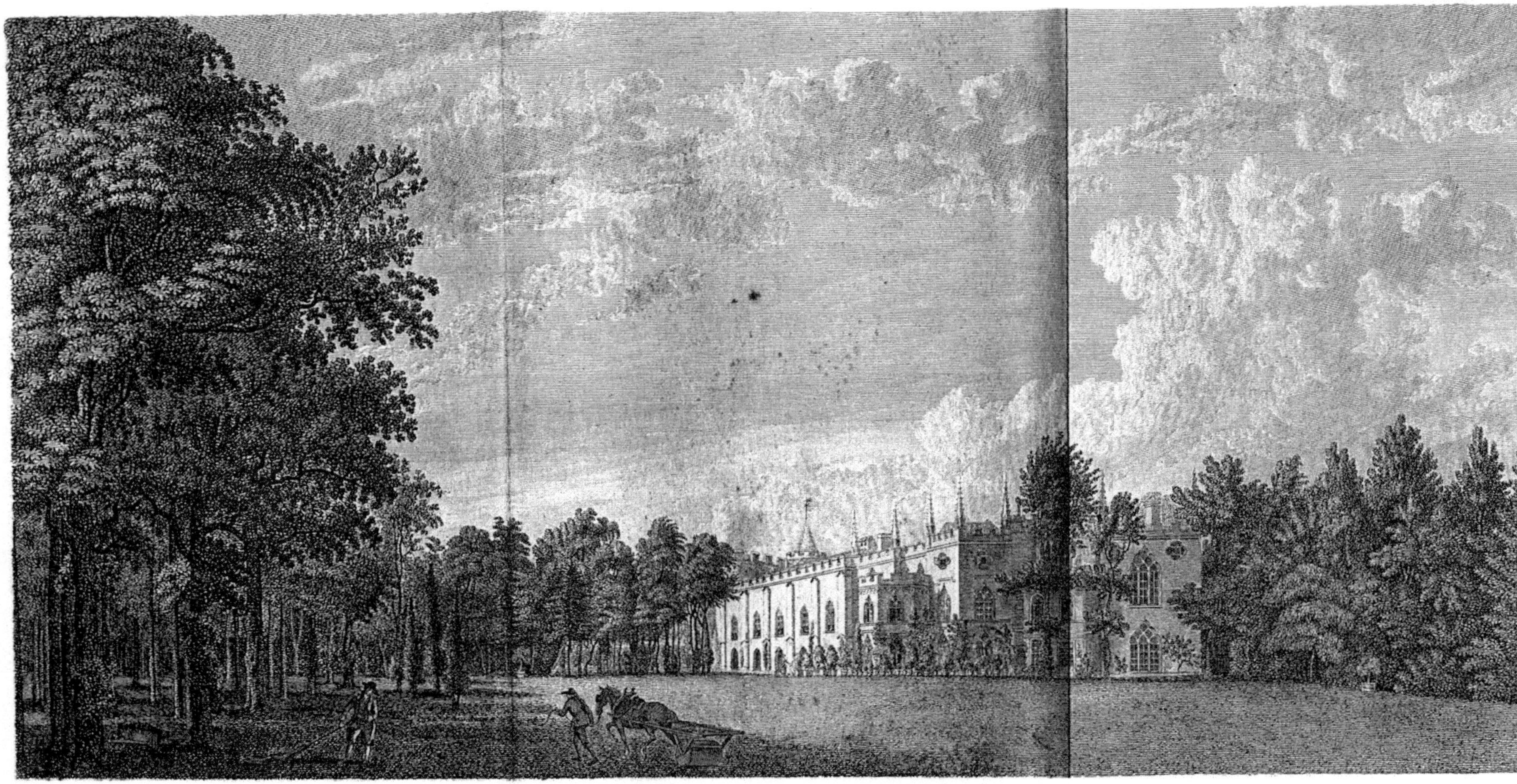

EAST FRONT OF STRAWBERRY HILL.

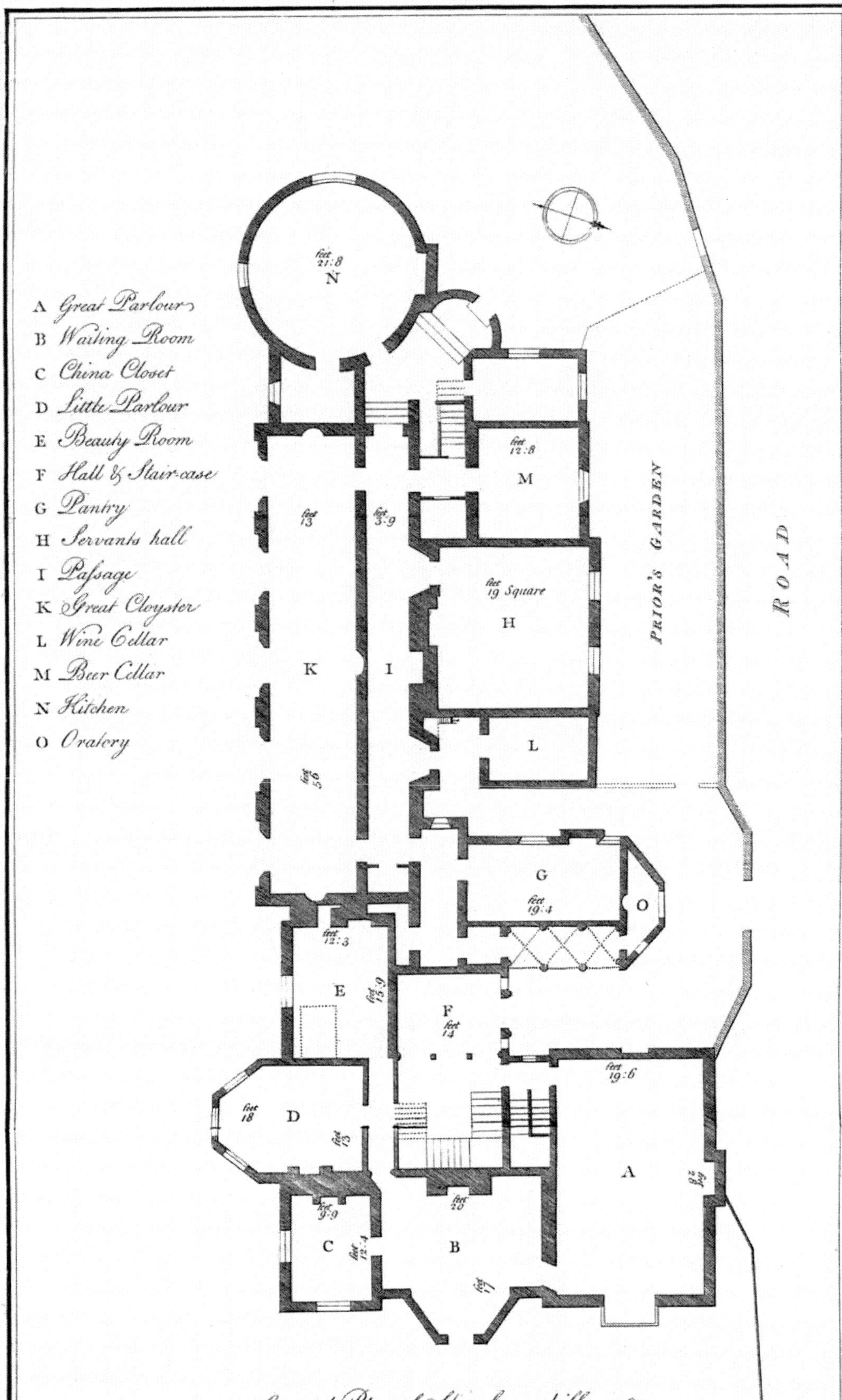

Ground Plan of Strawberry-hill. 1781.

Vol. II. Pl. IV. P. 532.

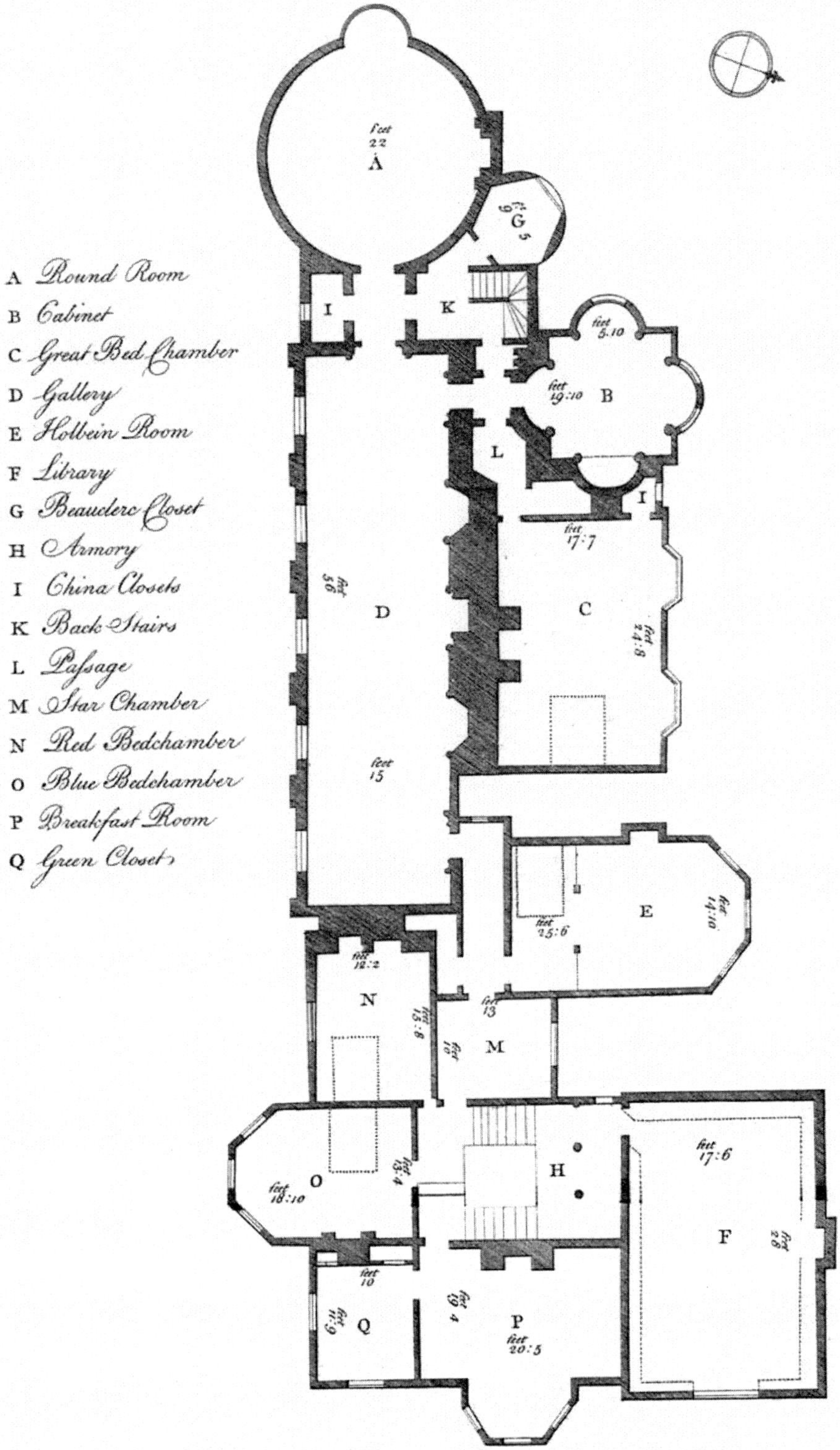

Principal Floor of Strawberry hill. 1781.

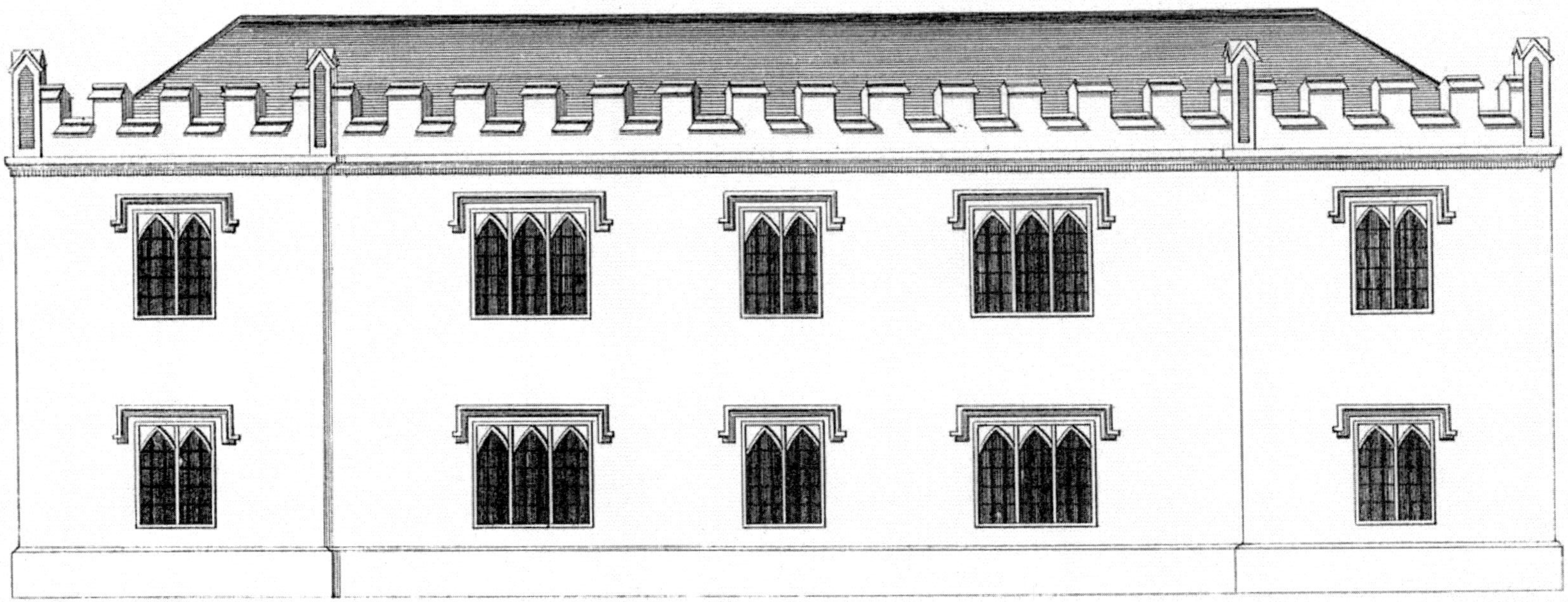

James Essex Delig. Barlow Sculp.

10 5 10 20 30 40 50

Offices

STRAWBERRY-HILL,

A BALLAD,

By WILLIAM PULTENEY Earl of Bath.

*To the tune of a former Song * written by* George Bubb Doddington lord Melcomb, *the burthen of which was, My Strawberry, my Strawberry ſhall bear away the Bell.*

I.

SOME cry up Gunnerſbury,
For Sion ſome declare ;
And ſome ſay that with Chiſwick-houſe
No villa can compare:
But aſk the beaux of Middleſex,
Who know the country well,
If Strawb'ry-hill, if Strawb'ry-hill
Don't bear away the bell ?

II.

Some love to roll down Greenwich-hill
For this thing and for that ;
And ſome prefer ſweet Marble-hill,
Though ſure 'tis ſomewhat flat :
Yet Marble-hill and Greenwich-hill,
If Kitty Clive † can tell,
From Strawb'ry-hill, from Strawb'ry-hill
Will never bear the bell.

* That ſong was written in praiſe of Mrs. Strawbridge, a lady with whom Mr. Doddington was in love.

† Mrs. Clive, the actreſs, lived near Strawberry-hill, in a houſe which Mr. Walpole bought and gave to her.

III.

Though Surry boaſts its Oatlands,
And Clermont kept ſo jim,
And ſome prefer ſweet Southcote's,
'Tis but a dainty whim;
For aſk the gallant Briſtow*,
Who does in taſte excell,
If Strawb'ry-hill, if Strawb'ry-hill
Don't bear away the bell?

IV.

Since Denham ſung of Cooper's,
There's ſcarce a hill around
But what in ſong or ditty
Is turn'd to fairy-ground——
Ah, peace be with their memories!
I wiſh them wondrous well;
But Strawb'ry-hill, but Strawb'ry-hill
Muſt bear away the bell.

V.

Great William † dwells at Windſor,
As Edward did of old,
And many a Gaul and many a Scot
Have found him full as bold.
On lofty hills like Windſor
Such heroes ought to dwell;
Yet little folks like Strawb'ry-hill,
Like Strawb'ry-hill as well.

The 2d, 4th and 5th ſtanzas were added by Mr. W.

* William Briſtow, eſq. brother of the counteſs of Buckingham, friend of lord Bath, and a great pretender to taſte.

† William duke of Cumberland.

LIST OF THE BOOKS

Printed at Strawberry-hill.

TWO Odes by Mr. Gray; quarto, 1757: 1000 copies.

Tranflation of part of Hentzner's Travels; fmall octavo, 1757: 220 copies.

Royal and Noble Authors; 2 vol. fmall oct. 1758: 300 copies.

Walpole's Fugitive Pieces; fmall oct. 1758: 200 copies.

Whitworth's Account of Ruffia; fmall oct. 1758: 700 copies.

Spence's Parallel of Magliabechi and Hill; fmall oct. 1758: 700 copies.

Bentley's Lucan; quarto, 1759: 500 copies.

Anecdotes of Painting; fmall quarto, 3 vol. and 1 of Engravers; 1761: 600 copies.

A fecond edition of the fame, 1765.

Lord Herbert's Life; fmall quarto, 1764: 200 copies.

Lady Temple's Poems, quarto, 1764: 100 copies.

Cornélie, Tragedie de Henaut; fmall octavo, 1768: 200 copies; 150 went to Paris.

The Myfterious Mother, Tragedy; fmall octavo, 1768: 50 copies.

Hoyland's Poems; fmall octavo, 1769: 300 copies.

Memoires de Grammont; ſmall quarto, 1771: 100 copies: 30 went to Paris.

Letters of Edward VI. ſmall quarto, 1771: 200 copies.

Miſcellaneous Antiquities, 2 numbers; ſmall quarto, 1772: 500 copies.

Deſcription of Strawberry-hill; ſmall quarto, 1774; 100 copies, 6 on large paper.

Mr. Fitzpatrick's Dorinda, and Mr. Charles Fox's Verſes to Mrs. Crewe; ſmall quarto, 1775: 300 copies.

The Sleep-walker, Comedy, by lady Craven; ſmall octavo, 1778: 75 copies.

Letter to the Editor of Chatterton's Miſcellanies; octavo, 1779: 200 copies.

Mr. Charles Miller's Verſes to lady Horatia Waldegrave; ſmall quarto, 1780: 150 copies.

Fourth volume of The Anecdotes of Painting, printed in 1770, but not publiſhed till October 1780: 600 copies.

Mr. Jones's Ode on lord Althorp's Marriage; ſmall quarto, 1781: 250 copies.

Letter from the hon. Thomas Walpole; ſmall quarto, 1781: 120 copies.

Deſcription of Strawberry-hill; royal quarto, 1784: 200 copies.

N. B. Mr. Miller's, Mr. Fitzpatrick's, and Mr. Fox's Verſes, Hoyland's Poems, and Mr. T. Walpole's Letter, were only looſe ſheets or ſmall tracts.

PALLAS ATHENE

More Walpoliana from Pallas Athene

Designs by Mr. R. Bentley for six poems by Mr. T. Gray

Commissioned by Walpole, this is one of the landmarks of English book design, with enchanting illustrations for six of Gray's most important poems, including the *Elegy in a Country Churchyard.*

The most graceful monument to gothic Rococo.
Kenneth Clark

ISBN 978 1 84368 058 1

On Modern Gardening

By a mile the most brilliant and most influential essay ever written on English garden history.
Tom Turner, Professor of Garden History, University of Greenwich

Walpole single-handedly determined (or distorted) the writing of landscape architecture history to this day.
John Dixon Hunt

ISBN 978 1 873429 83 9

Hieroglyphic Tales

These short tales can claim to be the first surrealist writings in English — and remain some of the strangest fictions in all literature. They were originally published in 1785 in an edition of six copies, all of which Walpole kept for himself.
With an extra story preserved only in manuscript, and an introduction by Kenneth Gross.

ISBN 978 1 84368 059 8

First published Strawberry Hill, 1774.
Second edition with illustrations, Strawberry Hill, 1784.
Third edition as part of *The Works of Horatio Walpole*, London 1798.

This edition published 2010 by Pallas Athene (Publishers) Ltd,
42 Spencer Rise, London NW5 1AP

www.pallasathene.co.uk

ISBN 978 1 84368 057 4

Publisher's Note

Walpole first published the *Description* in an edition of a hundred copies in 1774. Ten years later he published two hundred copies of an enlarged edition with twenty six illustrations. Of these, eighty copies were kept to be given to friends. There is no evidence that the *Description* was sold as a guidebook for visitors to the house: rather, it was intended to be a definitive account of the building, and catalogue of its contents. It was reprinted in Walpole's posthumously published *Works*, and it is this edition we have reproduced here. The pagination is that of the original volume, starting at p. 396, and the illustrations have been placed as closely as possible to the pages to which they refer.

Walpole also made extra-illustrated copies of the *Description*, into which drawings and further engravings of the works of art in his collection were inserted. It is the cover of one of these extra-illustrated copies that is reproduced on the cover of this volume, courtesy of the Lewis Walpole Library, Yale University.

Printed in England